The Misadventures of Mistress Soul

a life in France

Jan Hartley

Published by Linen Press, London 2020
8 Maltings Lodge
Corney Reach Way
London
W4 2TT

www.linen-press.com

Cover design: Ginny Fraser
Typeset by Zebedee Design.
Printed and bound by Lightning Source
ISBN 978-1-9996046-5-3

About the Author

London. 1940. A metal bed screen crashes down on the bed where Jan Hartley has just been born. That screen protects her and her mother from a blown and shattered window as a bomb drops into their garden. This momentous event becomes the chorus line of her life – relative calm broken by regular disasters. Aged two, she was sent away while her father fought in Egypt and her mother worked in a factory. Like many children, she escaped into the imaginary worlds of books. She still remembers them – their smell, and the feel of thin, greyish wartime paper. Books became her friends, her family, her therapy, her comfort, her education, her life, and the antidote to a difficult real one. She began to write – some pretty awful poems and dramatic, sentimental short stories, full of pain and longing. Then she wrote the blog that became this book. Now she looks back at the young Jan with a little love and a lot of forgiveness.

This book is dedicated to my family, Neil and Sara, Brian, Miles, Harley and Beth, and to my best friend, Gary.

Acknowledgements

Producing this book has involved the efforts of so many people, like Hugh and Bassie Scott who brought us to Languedoc, Johnny Brewer who helped to set up the blog site, and my faithful followers whose supportive comments sustained my blog throughout the years of its existence. There is, too, my cast of characters, friends old and new, whose contributions to my story are everything because my beautiful physical landscape would be barren without the people I love. Their support, and that of my family, in setting out on this potentially foolhardy venture, has sustained me. Thank you, everyone. And to my daughter, Sara, who has also fallen in love with Languedoc and visits whenever possible, I give my gratitude and my love.

Then I met Lynn Michell, writing group facilitator and publisher, whose encouragement and admiration of my memoir gave me a huge boost in confidence – in myself and in my writing. Whatever happens to this book, the adventure of writing it has done wonders for my self-esteem. Through Lynn, I connected with three young women who now know my book better than I do. The eagle-eyed Linen Press interns gave their time and expertise to polish this book to its shiny present. Thank you, Chania Fox and the two Sarahs, Hough and Cassidy, for your amazing work.

I don't know how to adequately express my admiration and gratitude to Ginny Fraser who spent many, many hours producing the front cover and the chapter illustrations. We owe you so much, Gin (and so much gin).

Then there is Techy Boy, The Husband, Gazzie, Gary. He laughs at my jokes, he undoes my computing errors, finds my lost pages, pre-warms the study where I write, warms my heart and feeds my soul. And can be jolly aggravating . . . but that's life and this book is a little window on that life. In stained glass.

Contents

Preface

May 2020

We closed the door on the last guest in our Bed and Breakfast, The Pearl Fisher, in Whitstable. I was seventy-five years old. It was time to retire. In the past fifteen years, Gaz and I had converted a Victorian House into a six bedroom guest house, and from very shaky beginnings had turned it into a successful business. We had saved enough to buy a two bedroom home, just up the road in Bungalow City.

Now free from Bedding and Breakfasting, and with time to spare, I fell back on my previous fantasies: appearing as the female lead on the West End Stage, winning *X Factor*, being a contestant on *Strictly Come Dancing*, writing a successful novel or even an unsuccessful one. Being published would do. But gradually reality dawned and I knew without a shadow of a doubt that these were . . . fantasies, out of reach for a woman of a certain age, and out of sight now.

'Oh, well,' I thought, 'I'll get on with the housework, mow the lawn, go to the doctor, think about and decide against going for a ten minute walk to the beach or a twenty minute walk into town because I might meet a dog. Or some other animal. They all frighten me.'

I had plenty of friends, and my daughter and grandchildren frequently visited. I belonged to a thriving monthly book club.

I tried a choir but couldn't reach the soprano notes and I liked that part so I left. Whitstable is known for its artistic community of painters, beaders, sculptors – just my sorta town. It has a great theatre, wonderful restaurants.

Every night at five o'clock a gentleman in a wheelchair trundled past the front of the bungalow, followed by his dog.

'That man in a wheelchair just went by,' I'd say to Gaz.

I felt as if I was living in God's Waiting Room. Without the discipline of having to make beds, take bookings, buy provisions, my life was freewheeling, albeit very slowly, out of my control. I began to accept that at my age, this was probably all that I could expect. Despite all the opportunities surrounding me, I was slipping, inevitably it seemed, towards senility. I even, can you believe, considered not dying my hair platinum blond and not wearing lots of make-up. Though patient, The Husband was beginning to get worried and constantly showed me advertisements for Zumba lessons, deep sea diving, potholing. Believe me, I was not that unhappy. Then why did I have that Peggy Lee song, 'Is That All There Is?', playing on a loop? What was I wanting, and missing? I was lucky, wasn't I? I had good friends, a loving family, and was living in the best town in England. I was fine. Wasn't I? I should be revelling in the rest from never-ending hard physical work as well as from being at the beck and call of guests. This was my time. We were far from rich, but we had enough to get by, if we were careful. I told myself I needed a good slap for being so ungrateful. But still . . .

One day there was a knock on my front door. No, not a Jehovah's Witness bringing Good News, but an old friend. She had left Whitstable to live in France eight years previously and had called to ask if we would be so kind as to house-cat-and-swimming-pool-sit for her for a fortnight in September. We promised her an answer in the following thirty seconds . . . I looked at Gaz, he looked at me. A spark of excitement fizzed between us.

'We'll, erm, have to re-arrange a few things,' I said, 'but, just as a favour, so you two can get away, we'll do it. Just for the two weeks, mind.'

1

What's French for divorce?

November 2017

What have I done?

At the end of the two week house-sitting stint in September, we signed up for a year's house rental in France, starting in December. What madness. I am 78 years old. My husband is 60 something. I choose to forget his exact age, OK? We had only just bought a bungalow in Seasalter (aka God's Waiting Room).

The future looked bleak and featureless.

And now here I am acting like a school leaver going on a gap year, preparing to leave my children and grandchildren, and travel to the ends of the earth, to the middle of nowhere, to . . . well . . . southern France. Not Provence, to be with Peter Mayle and footballers from Cheshire with a second home they visit once a year. No, Languedoc. Has anyone heard of it? Can anyone even say it? And there's another thing; the language in Languedoc. It's French, and the last time I said *oui* was in 1957 when I took my O levels.

We had three months to make a lifetime's arrangements, and the time went in a flash. We managed to rent our bungalow. We had long discussions with family and friends, suffered their worries and their tears and, not without trepidation, started making the final preparations. Suddenly the departure date was only a few weeks away and stress etched its ugly lines upon our brows,

Normally, The Husband and I have a row about once every three years. From this point in the adventure until we arrived in France, we had them daily, mainly about the fact that I wanted, nay needed, to take every item of clothing I owned. We sent three large cases ahead and filled the car. Divorce proceedings were mooted on more than one occasion.

The last unresolved issues were all car-related so we booked our Kia Soul – Rocky Soul because of her jazzy interior – in for her service and MOT.

Now Rocky had always liked a little trip to our nearest town, but obviously this longer journey – across the Channel and six hundred and fifty miles through France – was causing her some problems because she started throwing spanners in her works. Occasionally, she refused to let her door handle be used so that it flapped uselessly in our hands. She started skidding a bit to tell us that her tyres needed changing. She was so temperamental we started a more formal name-calling to try to bring her in line: Mistress R. Soul.

Because of her shocking misbehaviour, the MOT and tyre change took a day and a half, while we rested like huge cuckoos in our friends' house. Finally the Car Doctor rang to say everything had been done, but the key had broken.

'Bring spare key,' he said.

'We don't have one,' said we. 'It mysteriously disappeared.'

The garage quoted us two weeks and £300! We were booked to go two days later. Car Doctor got two keys done for £80.

We had had our house in France booked since September. While cuckooing, we received a text: *Your soon-to-be landlady has had a mild stroke and your future accommodation is in doubt.* Poor woman. Poor us. I bawled and bawled. We were homeless in two countries at once. Clever, even for us. However, Masterful Husband, the Bear Grylls of the five star hotel world (he could survive anywhere, given a bit of luxury) said, 'We are still goin' woman! Get yer toe nails painted.'

Our fourth *au revoir*[1] party (note: already picking up the language) was a surprise from our daughter and her husband. They had gathered together old friends who now, for some strange reason, all sported moustaches, berets, striped jumpers and strings of onions. I personally like a gal with a moustache, but that's another story. They treated us to a typical French meal and we drank French wine. By the end of the evening, our language had improved no end. Not French language, but then Rome wasn't built in a day, and anyway, that's in Italy. Actually all language had deteriorated by bedtime, truth be told. And it will be.

Early on the morrow, we left for Dover. The hill from our daughter's house was like an ice rink.

'But,' said Explorer Husband, 'we might face worse than this, old girl, hang on to yer hat!' We were down in no time.

'I'll just check the tyres at the garage. Extra weight on, you know.'

'That sort of hilarious rejoinder will surely get you on the stage, my dear,' I replied icily.

---

1 Goodbye

I ignored the slur and continued with my *Speak French in One Easy Lesson* tape. The Husband's face, red and rather unattractive, appeared in the windscreen, calling me out into the cold. Sighing, I joined him.

'The air thingy, instead of pumping air in, has sucked it all out. And now it's broken.'

Son in law, SuperBri, was with us in ten minutes, mended it in another ten, and sent us on our way.

At Dover, a smiling girl came to the car. 'All on time,' she said, waving us through. Our eager little smiles faded a bit by the time we boarded the train two hours later. But we were on our way!

Incidentally, the French word for divorce is the same. *Divorce.*

2

This trip may be the Rouen of us

December 2017

Despite the two hour delay at Le Shuttle, we made good time through northern France towards our first stopping point in Alençon where we were due at 7.00 pm. The skies were grey, but a little of the excitement filtered through as we drove through rather British scenery and very French buildings.

'Whatever happens,' The Husband said, 'we don't want to go through Rouen.'

We went through Rouen – and I began to understand his concern as I navigated us into the town. And up the town. And down the town. And round the town. We drove for two whole hours right through the evening rush hour. So slow was our progress that people began to recognise us and to wave cheerily at our glum faces as we circulated yet again. And again.

Finally, Miles our Satnav stopped sulking and brought us to a long driveway running though parkland dotted with deer, and there was the chateau, scene of our first stopover on the journey. No castle-like crenellations, just a beautifully proportioned house of black slate roofs and grey stone walls.

The Marquis Hervé Glicout les Touches and his wife the Marchioness-and-Chef met us and showed us to our room. It was very old and rather beautiful. The whole place was steeped in history and the decor matched the era. We were the only guests and, following *apéritifs*[1] and *amuse-bouches*[2] in front of the fire with Herv, as we now called him, we were served a four course meal in a candlelit dining room with Chopin Nocturnes playing in the background.

Gary and I looked at each other incredulously. We had driven from our daughter's home in England and eight hours later we were in another world, a world of gavottes and quadrilles, of horse-drawn carriages and crinolines, of a before-the-revolution time of the privileged few. Trying not to let our social conscience interfere, we graciously thanked our hosts and glided up to a bedroom of faded *Toile de Jouy* wallpaper and hand-embroidered sheets. Yup, this was the life to which I could become accustomed.

When we woke on the morrow our dreams of powdered wigs and beauty patches still cobwebbed us as we processioned to the Orangery for our first French breakfast. It seemed ungracious to enquire whether the oranges for the jam were from the beautiful glass building in which we breakfasted, but the cheese was local, the croissants so light they seemed to float, and the coffee was as dark as Satan's soul. And to top it all were the 'heggs from our own 'ens,' as Herv said. And jolly l'oeufly they were too.

Boarding Mistress R. Soul after fond farewells was slightly

---

1 Drink

2 Appetiser

disappointing, for we were rather expecting a carriage and pair, but we were grateful for her diva-esque behaviour as rain continued to turn the roads into rivers while we stayed mainly warm and dry inside. We gave a little wiggle to shake off the past and slowly pressed the accelerator into the future.

3

Turrets and troglodytes

December 2017

One of the propositions The Husband laid before me was that our journey to the Promised Land would take us through the Loire Valley. I had seen photos and paintings of this area with its gleaming black turrets set atop white castles, exactly like the fairy tale palace one imagined as a child, and I was eager to see the reality,

Despite continuing skies of endless grey, a mean rain and traffic spray, I saw only beauty. If anything, the deluge made it more glorious as it slicked turrets to an iridescent glory and washed terraces and columns, the shrubs and trees, as if preparing the scene to be its best for our arrival.

We headed for the spectacular caves of the troglodytes, built into the tufa limestone cliffs. For hundreds of years they were used by local dwellers, with many still in use today for wine storage because they are cool in summer and warm in winter. A few are even used as dwellings. To be honest, the caves looked a good deal cosier than the austere beauty of some of the palaces.

There was, apparently, an area where actors put on performances showing how the cave dwellers lived. However, I try to avoid the W word (walking) as much as possible and as that was the only way to get to the performance area, we didn't go. I am sure it was fascinating.

I know, I know. I should be a responsible citizen who walks. In my defence, I ask you, if God had wanted us to walk everywhere, why did he invent cars? You can't argue with that.

My aversion to the W word means we didn't do as much as we should. For instance, the Museum of Mushrooms looked fascinating, but the trudge across the field to reach it did not, so we passed by the famous fungi and continued southwards. To be fair, it had been very wet and cold, but even through a car window it is obvious that the Loire more than deserves its reputation for beauty. It is a stunning place.

Our second hotel, in Chinon, was even older than the previous chateau but recently restored with amazing modern amenities like a wonderful bathtub. This B&B, inexplicably not a hotel, was called Au Relais Saint Maurice. Now the owner was also called Maurice and he was justifiably proud of this beautiful building. I longed to ask him if he had been Sainted and what for, but it seemed a bit personal, so I held my tongue. But I'm telling you this for nowt, if it was for services to the hospitality industry, then it was well-deserved.

It was a sad but beautiful town that greeted us as we tentatively trod the rain-shiny cobbles of Chinon in search of sustenance. The population had taken to the shadows and the place was empty, but we found a lovely old, red-painted restaurant and raised our glasses to the unknown future.

The Christmas decorations in the Relais owed a lot to Mr

Dickens: a long table dressed in red and gold, fairy lights twinkling everywhere, fern-swagged stairs and an enormous Christmas tree, decorated to within an inch of its pine-scented life, set beside a roaring log fire. And all this was to set the stage for breakfast with cinnamon toast, honey, oranges and eggs sporting jolly Christmas hats.

I wouldn't have been surprised if that annoying child Tiny Tim had joined us with a goose stuck under his arm.

As an aside, if you're going to call your baby boy Tiny Anything, he's not going to have a very aspirational life. On the other hand, there's Big Boris. Now there's a name to launch a child to greatness.

4

Getting the Abbey habit

December 2017

The next leg of our journey was a four hour drive to Montauban. We try very hard to avoid motorways and had lovely journeys across rolling hills and fields as green as very green things. (Some say my adjectival acumen is second to none.)

We had been warned many times about leaving our car in an unsupervised spot:

1) because of the English number plates

2) because it was full of luggage.

Now I did wonder what any self-respecting robber would want with four suitcases of very large clothes, but we heeded the warnings. After all, we might have overlooked this aspect of French culture i.e. a desire, in the French demi-monde, to dress in big frocks. We realised we didn't know a lot about such things. However, finding a restaurant with windows overlooking the car park and near enough for us to rush out and kill the thieves with plastic forks proved impossible . . . so we stopped eating unless Mistress R. Soul was safely locked away.

With the help of Miles Satnav, we found our next hotel, Abbaye des Capucins, which very roughly translates as Monkey Abbey. Checked in. Nice place. Bit arty. Bit of a Christmas vibe.

Having read on Trip Advisor about their four star restaurant, I said (in French) to Reception Man,

'And a table for two this evening?'

'*Mais non,*' says he, '*nous sommes complet.*' We are full.

I threw myself on the floor, crying. 'Why are all the fates against me? I don't ask for much in life, just a table for two. God, whyyyyyy haasst thouuuu forsaken meeeeeeee?'

Peering over the reception desk, Reception Man said, 'But, Madame, tonight we have a fashion party, with free food and as much champagne as you can drink, and then a disco. All of which you are welcome to attend as our guest.'

Gathering up my clothes and my dignity, I rose from the floor. 'Well, we may,' I said haughtily.

Me and The Husband walked away, heads held high . . . to prepare for the evening.

We were one of the first to arrive. Got a table. Charming waitress brought champagne and an amazing array of canapés and oysters. We soon realised it was some sort of networking party, and that, 'Hi, we're Jan and Gary on holiday from England,' did not cut it with the contact-hungry delegates. They slunk away from us like disappointed hyenas finding a carcass already picked clean.

The fashion show was about thirty minutes of obviously amateur models of about sixteen in very skimpy underwear. We never did find out what it was all about. But we did have a lot of food, a lot of wine and a lot of fun.

The following morning, as we made our breakfast selection, we discovered the reason for last evening's full restaurant. There was a team of rugby players staying at the hotel. They came in to breakfast like a team of gladiators, the most magnificent examples of manhood you have ever seen.

'Ahh,' I sighed dreamily, giving my breakfast egg a merry little thwack.

As if to punish my lasciviousness, the egg, which I had imagined to be hard boiled, was, in fact, raw and shot its contents into my eyes, over my top and over one of the passing gladiators. Rather unkindly, I thought, he pushed my hand away when I tried to mop him down. Gary pulled me quickly away to prevent causing further uproar and, without finishing our breakfasts, we slunk up to our room.

After a quick shower and change of clothes, we packed for the last leg of our journey. We were to stay with our friends and their three big dogs (eek) until we knew the situation with our landlady after her stroke, and when (or if) we could move to our new French home.

After all that has happened over the last few weeks, The Husband and I have the most God-awful colds, no doubt due to the stresses and strains of the preparations and the journey. Admittedly there have been many moments when I decided the entire plan was ill-conceived and foolhardy in the extreme. But, as I lie here in my bed in Gabian, looking out at a cloudless blue sky, I think maybe it will, at the very least, be OK.

5

A strangulation of Santas

December 2017

It's not the same though is it? In France? Some *dinde* and some *gui* sounds more like two types of poisonous herb than turkey and mistletoe. I know we are supposed to be embracing the culture of our temporarily adopted country, but you can't muck about with Christmas.

I don't know about 'Deck the Halls' but if they are decking, it ain't showin'. In the supermarket there are only a few deflated balloons hanging sadly like leftovers from a Pride march.

Where are the turkeys, the mince pies, the after-office parties with drunken Santas lying in the gutters? It's just not festive, is it? The sparkle of Christmas is on dimmer. Added to which, the skies are so bloody blue, you daren't sit in front of a window to read in case your book catches fire. Yesterday Gaz was sunbathing in shorts and sun cream. Mind you, he drops his clothes if someone switches on a light.

Here we are cuckooing again and waiting for news of our putative landlady and her poor heart. Kind as our friends are, it's hard not to feel down. I am a homemaker. I like to be in my own place, with my own things around me. I like to know whether or not to flush the toilet at night. I like to be an occasional slob. I like watching things *I* want to watch on the television, by a log fire, with The Husband. And, yes, of course I know that there are people far worse off than me and I'm acting like a spoiled child, but I'm not well. We are both still whirling cauldrons of catarrh and infection. Sitting in bed we cough like a couple of ninety-year-old, sixty-a-dayers. Me in curlers and a winceyette nightie, him in a moth-eaten jumper. Ah, the romance of our French sojourn.

To all those who said they envied this adventure, listen up. We are still homeless. I am having the worst cold of my entire life. English TV is an hour later here. I can't watch *Have I Got News for You* at 10 o'clock because that's bedtime. We're not able to record a programme and change channels at the same time. If someone sneezes in the next village, we lose our TV signal for the whole evening. The internet connection is so poor that I cannot listen to a complete radio play. There are now five whodunits with the whodunit character frustratingly still unknown to me.

Bear with me while I rant on. The bread's too crusty. The sausages are white, and don't get me started on the bacon. You can't get Marmite or peanut butter or Oxo. Turkey is rarely on sale and costs a Queen's Ransom. And listen to this – you can't get marmalade. The word marmalade comes from the French *Marie est malade*[1] because Queen Mary was given oranges to cure her sea sickness. You can't get frozen Yorkshires. On Christmas Day they eat *chapon* or capon – that's male chickens and, like a lot of males, they are tough and tasteless. Chickens, on the other hand, are the size of emaciated sparrows and the colour of bananas. Butchers display parts of an animal which should never, under any circumstances, be seen outside a body. Who, unless they are on the point of starvation, chooses to eat chicken gizzards? And please tell me this: why do the patisserie and cake sections in supermarkets need a whole shop to themselves? And yet . . . where are the overweight French? How does that happen?

My mood is matched by the Santas that hang from balcony railings in their thousands and look a little weary from struggling to get into houses with their sacks on their backs. Instead of being a jolly Christmas symbol, they look as if they've been hanged for crimes against good taste.

The Christmas trees remain pristine as if even the most eager of vandals find little excitement in stealing silver paper bows. Instead, the mischievous wind has taken the decorations which cling to our legs as we wander the streets.

Despite all of which . . . there is a joy in showing off our new homeland. On the afternoon of New Year's Eve, we took visiting friends to Bouzigues for a seafood lunch and to watch people fall in the sea. We sat under blue skies, staring at sparkling water. In the evening we shared with our friends a *salmon en croute*[2] from Picard, an up-market frozen food chain. We played a hand or two of Nomination Whist and were all, save one, in bed by ten. The Husband raised a lonely glass to Jools Holland

1 Marie is ill
2 Salmon baked in pastry

on TV and waited the one hour time difference for Jools to raise one back. I think I'll forsake the rather austere nomenclature of The Husband because Gazzie is more like his old self now that we are *almost* settled.

There is good news! On Friday, we will move into our temporary adopted home where our lovely daughter will come to visit in early January. I can't wait to show her my immersion in the customs and culture of our new country.

And here we are in our own house! We have our own front door. We are unpacked and the fire's alight. The fridge is full. The Christmas trees are up and dressed. We are like two world-weary animals who have finally reached their home territory. We curl up before the roaring fire, watch TV, and recover from the slings and arrows of outrageous misfortune that have brought us to this point, and search for the *joie de vivre*[3] that we lost somewhere along the way.

2018 has, without our help, arrived. To our family and friends we send our sincerest wishes for your good health and happiness over the next year. And to us, to Gazzie and me? Rather apprehensively we turn towards a future which will take us out of our comfort zone and into unknown territory. Hold on tight. It could be a bumpy ride.

---

3 Joy of life

6

Flamingo blues

January 2018

Our daughter, Sara, has arrived so we are going to explore in earnest – no, we haven't changed the name of the car or the mode of transport. We decided on Narbonne and its seaside partner, Gruissan, as being easily achievable in one day, even after we'd factored in the necessary ninety-minute refreshment break.

Narbonne is a pretty town of ancient, honey-coloured buildings and well-loved and tended waterways. It is linked to the Canal du Midi and the Aude River by the Canal de la Robine which runs through the centre of town. There has been a settlement here since 118 BC. Narbonne Cathedral, still one of the tallest churches in France, was never finished, the reasons being many, but the most important is that the completed cathedral would have required the demolition of the city wall. Given that the fourteenth century brought the plague, knocking down the protective city walls seemed like a bad idea. None of these dangers, however, prevented the births of Narbonne's famous son, the singer Charles Trenet, and that very strange saint, Sebastian.

We chose Gruissan for our refreshment break because it is on the coast. A big water sports area in the summer, at the beginning of January it is somewhat more subdued with the wild birds reclaiming the land and swooping down annoyingly at us, the interlopers. I saw my first flamingoes. In the cold, they looked more blue than pink. They were each standing miserably on one leg. Trying to keep the other out of the freezing water, I suppose. In fact we saw one fall over. Trying to warm both feet at once?

Gruissan is famous for two things. The first is that there are one thousand three hundred wooden houses standing on stilts. It looked like some ghostly Atlantis: grey wooden shacks that had risen from the depths of the ocean with seaweed fanning out from the stilts like shredded stockings. The wooden shutters banged and the wind howled through the empty streets.

Its other claim to fame is, and I quote Wikipedia here: 'the home of Gary W. Harvey the reputed inventor of time travel using the 'magnetic pulse resonance theory' to excite atoms into a single vibration direction at previously thought unachievable speeds. His sudden disappearance is thought by many to be the result of a 'journey that went wrong'.

On Friday last, on an early January morning, we ate breakfast in the garden. It was twenty-two degrees and sunny. We went for lunch with our friends from Gabian at La Maison in nearby Tourbes and ate the best food we'd had since we arrived. And not an oyster in sight! Yippee! We could see Sara gradually being seduced by Languedoc and to ensure frequent return visits, we proposed a visit to the university town of Montpellier on the way to the airport. Another beautiful, buzzy city with great Christmas decorations (last mention, I promise).

Gazzie had done his homework this time. On the previous trip to the airport, to collect Sara, we had got terribly lost, leaving her waiting for an hour. This time we parked on the outskirts of town and caught a tram into the centre. The trams are amazingly beautiful, painted in bright colours and designs by Christian Lacroix. The cost for three return tram fares and five hours parking? Just under five euros. What!

Lordy, Lordy, we walked so much yesterday around Gruissan and Narbonne that my legs were two inches shorter this morning. And now we were treading every inch of the cobbled streets of old Montpellier. Did I moan? Did I say, 'Gazzie, can we please get a taxi back to the car?' Yes, I damn well did. Did he listen? No, he damn well didn't.

He did allow us our refreshment break, though, and we chose our restaurant solely by its name. *Comme un dimanche sous le figuier*. Translated: Like a Sunday under the fig tree. It was wonderfully quirky inside.

The tough part, dear friends, the very worst, was saying goodbye. Tears were shed at Sara's departure. We drove out of the airport with heavy hearts and snively noses. Comfort, in the shape of a little glass of wine, some crusty bread and really smelly cheese, was forsworn to us because of our resolution on New Year's Eve to give up such bacchanalian excess. After a few miles of silence, the jolly little lights of a roadside supermarket flashed provocatively into the dark interior of our homesick souls. He looked at me. I looked at him. Mistress R. Soul hesitated and questioningly shuddered to a stop. We slowly released our seat belts and opened our doors.

7

Vive la différence!

January 2018

I know that I have, how shall I say, extracted liquid from the urinary tract of France in previous chapters, but time has lent me a more balanced view, I think. Whoever said, 'Comparison is odious,' is right. To compare France with the UK is pointless. They are very different and thank goodness for that. For me, though, the familiar is safe and the unfamiliar is a bit scary. I am not a great explorer, seeking new lands and new experiences. I merely want to familiarise myself with the unfamiliar.

In order to decode some of the unfamiliarities, we started French conversation classes this week. School is the small dining room at our teacher's home where we are closely observed by her three cats. In our first week, our fellow students were three Brits and an Australian, all of us over sixty. Some of us, well over. Of course, only French may be spoken. On that first day, the cats said more than either Gaz or me. The last part of the session is when students read their work out loud. Kevin, the Aussie, read a fifteen minute piece, in pretty perfect French, philosophising about his partner's visit to the A&E department of a Paris hospital, quoting, still in French, *Macbeth*, *King Lear* and Dylan Thomas. This is the Intermediate class!

And another decode is to familiarise ourselves with our local area. I tell you, dear friends, it is not an arduous task. I know I should be donning walking boots and sporting a Tyrolean hat and setting off into the countryside on foot, but my goodness that walking gear is so . . . mmm . . . well, damned ugly. You can see just as much through a car window. And what sights there are to see. This area keeps giving beauty: old stone villages, cobbled streets and chateaux in abundance give way to rolling hills, blue in the distance, and pastures of succulent green-ness. And so with our souls fully prepared for artistic overload, we set out.

There is an easy walk, we are told, from our house to the village of Margon. As responsible tour guides, however, we thought we should take a drive along the route to make sure it was safe. As we slowly rolled on, windows down, a beautiful young lady with eyelashes to die for kept us company on the road alongside us. At the crossroads she brayed her goodbyes and we regretfully stroked her mane and watched her trot off.

Having driven right through the small village of Margon – and how is it every single village is painted with the pretty brush? – we could not stop. Some Siren was calling to us to drive deeper and deeper into the landscape ahead. It was early January and the sky was that particular pale blue that shades into silver when illuminated by a pale sun. We opened the car windows to air that was newly warm, fragranced by fresh grass and young vines.

We planted our carbon footprints over mile after mile of vineyards (so much wine, so little time) and on up into the mountains, past the chateaux, their turrets glinting black against the sky. The terrain grew wilder the higher we drove, with white water streams surging over granite boulders and bursting into scintillating parabolas. The ghostly shouts of last summer's canoeists and white water rafters echoed round us in the thin, quiet air.

We drank coffee outside in the hillside town of Roquebrun, famed for its Mimosa Fair in February, its Mediterranean Garden and, well, for just being so damned beautiful. Looking down on the white-foamed water jumping and tumbling through the valley below, I smiled contentedly and silently thanked my lucky stars that I had never, in the whole of my long life, had the least desire to don a wetsuit.

8

Pearls before swine

January 2018

I find him standing there, dagger in hand, blood dripping from his thumb to the floor. His head is bowed, not in submission, but almost in expectation. Of what? The honour that is his due? For what? I must say, it has been an epic battle, of Cap'n Ahab and Moby Dick proportions. So what is he hoping for? The Victoria Cross? The Legion d'Honneur? The Congressional Medal?

He drops to one knee, as if to be knighted for his bravery in . . . opening a damned oyster. I try to be kind and say, 'Arise, Sir Gaz,' but he cannot for the dagger has fallen and anchored his trousers to the floor.

While he is there, I begin to think about the whole subject of oysters. My personal opinion is that they are, along with most shellfish, the biggest marketing con in the world. All that trouble to open them and you are presented with something which looks like a piece of rubber in mucous. Aficionados are swallowers or biters. Swallowers throw back their heads, open their throats and there goes the oyster, never touching a taste bud. Biters cover the oyster in shallot vinegar, Tabasco sauce, chorizo, anything to mask the taste. Oh and then there are the ones who nag, 'Mind you don't spill the precious liquor from the shell.' It's seawater, people. You spill it – there are several large oceans to get spares from.

When a growing number of people began to suspect they were being fooled, new claims were made for these inedibles. The strongest, still rife today, is that they are an aphrodisiac. No proof of this has been found. And lord knows, Gazzie keeps trying them out. And the chances of finding a pearl? 1 in 12,000.

Thinking of eating that many oysters reminds me of another rite of passage beloved by shell food seekers. Picture a seaside hotel breakfast room. Person arrives tinged in green. He has that look that says he has just survived the initiation ceremony to an exclusive club. 'Up all night. Sick as a dog. Rogue oyster,' he says, with ill-concealed pride. There are looks of ill-concealed jealousy on some breakfasters' faces. Horror on others. Bizarre.

In this lovely part of France, nearly all restaurants sell *coquillages,* shellfish, in some form or other. The pretty seaside town of Mèze, for instance, has maybe a dozen restaurants around the harbour which only serve seafood. It is worth noting that in the UK a dozen oysters cost the best part of £25. Here it's €10. It is food (if you can call it such) for all, not for the few. So there is not the slightest excuse for pretension. When we visited Mèze, on a sunny Sunday lunchtime in January, most people were eating oysters and mussels. I can just about tolerate mussels in a garlic and cream sauce, but I eat with my eyes closed because once, when I did look at what was inside the shell, it looked exactly like the chopped-off ear of a hairy gnome.

Whilst I would still, almost, prefer to take a five minute W word than eat an oyster, to please my husband and daughter on her next visit we shall visit the Tarbouriech restaurant on the Étang de Thau near Marseillan. It is in a beautiful position overlooking the bay and so successful, humane and environmentally aware are the Tarbouriech family that their internationally-awarded seafood has been named after them. Tarbouriech oysters are prized the world over, particularly the Pink Diamond. Enough. They are oysters still.

9

You, you're drivin' me crazy

January 2018

We have taken to travelling incognito. It is a matter of life or death, dear friends. We're wearing striped jerseys, short black satin skirts with side splits – in which Gaz looks particularly fetching – berets and a string of onions. Nobody would recognise us as British. We start lots of conversations with, 'Listen, I shall only say zees once.' Honestly, I do believe we could fool anyone.

We have rubbed mud over Mistress R. Soul's number plates and she has a big sign on her back which reads: 'Don't blame us. We voted Remain.' Oh bugger, that's a giveaway. We wrote it in English. Note to self: Find Google Translate when we get home.

The reason for the subterfuge is that we face death or serious injury every time we venture out in the car. We are particular targets on roundabouts. Gazzie follows French road law by keeping to the inside lane, signalling his intention to be there, then signalling right to come out of the lane at his exit when he's ready. Suddenly there are three or four puce-faced drivers with not a signalling finger amongst them, inches, nay centimetres from our car, blowing their horns, gesticulating – I think that particular gesture is universal – while we just stop dead in confusion which causes more chaos, more anger, more fear.

There is also, apparently, a code known only to born and bred French people which tells them the direction to take when the signs you've been following for ten miles (times eight and divide by five for kilometres) suddenly disappear and you've driven so many times round the roundabout looking for an exit, you run out of petrol. Even more very angry people.

Then we have the fully automatic petrol stations.

'Oh, my goodness, what shall we do? It's all in French. Don't understand.'

'Calm down. It's all quite simple.'

'Diesel? What's the French for diesel? What's the French for petrol?'

And then, on checking our credit card statement some time later, we find thirty euros of petrol has cost one hundred and fifty euros. After a sleepless night, first thing in the morning, we ring the credit card company. OK. So here is the system. The multi-zillion pounds/euros profit-earning petrol company is so afraid that the little guy is going to think of a way to take more petrol than he has paid for, that it charges a one hundred and twenty euros pre-authorisation on the credit card. This amount can take up to twenty days to be repaid. How can this be legal?

Today we are ordering our Senior Citizen Railcards.

10

Earth hath not anything to show more fair
January 2018

Under the disguise previously described, we bravely set off once more, because there are so many beautiful, historic, unspoilt places to visit within a reasonable car journey from here.

Gary meticulously planned a trip to La Petite Camargue. Our first stop was in La Grande Motte. I love this town and disagree with those who say the buildings have not stood up well against the ravages of time. It was built in the 60s and 70s to a design by Jean Balladur who was inspired by the lost Mayan civilisation and devoted nearly thirty years of his life to the project. Today the town welcomes over two million tourists every year.

After wandering around, lost in admiration at what the town offers, we moved on to the wild and wonderful beaches at Le Grau-du-Roi. There is an untouched beauty to these resorts in winter and on a windy, overcast day in January, we braved the beach to look back to La Grande Motte. The sun illuminated the white buildings while around us a storm gathered, bending the sea grass flat against the sand and forming a legion of white horses on the waves.

We had lunch on the red and white gingham table cloths of Les Capucins Restaurant in the town square within the medieval city walls of Aigues-Mortes, of which I shall write later. Afterwards we walked along a canal lined with bone white, coppiced plane trees looking like calcified limbs against a pale blue sky.

Gary had planned our day to perfection. He knows the area because when he was hitchhiking as a student, he was picked up outside Paris by three students of Romany heritage. They drove him all the way through France, feeding him and sleeping alongside him on beaches. When they got into the Camargue, they invited him to a family wedding in Saintes-Marie-de-la-Mer.

In order to get to Saintes-Marie, we had to cross the Petit Rhône canal on the Bac du Sauvage or ferry boat. Completely free, the ferry plies its trade every half an hour during daylight hours. On a Wednesday in January, Gaz and I and Mistress R. Soul were the only passengers. The town is purported to be the capital of the Camargue, and certainly the spiritual home of Europe's gypsies, *les gitans*. Of course, out of season, almost everything was closed and the town was deserted, apart from a group of elderly gentlemen who played a spirited game of *boules*, mufflered up against the sea breeze.

We definitely want to return, possibly in May when gypsies

41

from all over Europe gather for their annual festivities. The town is dominated by huge statues of bulls and horses, animals which are central to the lives of the people of the Camargue.

As we drove deeper into the countryside, we passed the *manades* that are a feature of this area. Literally, *manades* are groups of semi-feral horses and cattle. The name has come to also mean the 'farms' or 'ranches' where visitors can stay and take part in the lives of the *gardians* or 'cowboys of the Camargue'.

We started to make our way home as a fierce orange sun began its own journey towards the horizon. The wetlands around us tck tck tickered and slippy-slithered with wildlife preparing for night – some settling down quietly whilst their nocturnal neighbours prepared to hunt.

Behind the swathes of golden reeds, the white Camarguaise horses snickered and pawed the soft ground. Huge black bulls looked over their fences to see who had the temerity to disturb their twilight rituals.

And then, impossibly, a starling murmuration swept over the car and across the marshland. The air around us stirred to the beat of a thousand wings and for a moment we were in dark shadow as they passed before the dying sun. With windows open, it seemed to us that we, alone in all the world, at that precious moment, were privileged to be part of the greatest show on earth. We could not speak. There was no need. We had shared a day that had shown us the best that man and nature can offer. The memory will be there for us when man and nature are at their worst.

And then we will say, 'Remember?'

11

Deliverance

February 2018

I have pondered, while we have been here, why so many ancient buildings in France remain in such good condition and I can only assume that the temperate weather is kinder to slate and stone than our own sometimes cruel conditions. In almost every town and village, history surrounds us in the narrow, cobbled streets where ancient buildings sit majestically alongside the rather squat and ugly newcomers. It is a joy to wander through them.

Certain villages are categorised as 'The Most Beautiful in France'. When we were here last September, we visited the village of Olargues. It most certainly deserves its place in that august company. High in the hills beyond Béziers, its cobbled streets are almost vertical in places, clinging on to the hillside overlooking the River Jaur.

On another warm January lunchtime, with good friends, we ate at the exquisite restaurant Fleurs d'Olargues overlooking the river. After we had moved upwind of the kitchen's freshly manured gardens, we were once more rendered speechless by the beauty of our surroundings, the excellent food and the very fine wine.

Based on the success of that visit, we decided to set out to Lagrasse. It was naive to think that a *'plus beau village'*[1] would be as *beau* on a grey day in January as on a warm, sunny day in September, but as already demonstrated, we do err on the side of naivety. Lagrasse is to be found high up in the Aude. Renowned for its Corbières wine, it is now home to numerous pottery workers and artists, and hosts many cultural and intellectual festivals such as *Le Banquet du Livre*.[2] On the day of our visit, Lagrasse was shut. Obviously its natural beauty is enhanced by the sun which shines, we are told, 360 days of the year, but not on a grey day in January. Shops, restaurants, church and school all had an air of cobwebbed waiting. Silence pressed against our ears as we tiptoed around the town. The lovely old buildings regarded us with shuttered disinterest. Faded signs promised fine wines, tapas, artisan-ware. Posters promised poetry, music and fun. But the village was in hibernation and we felt guilty for disturbing its winter sleep.

We found the car, carefully closed the doors, and started the engine so that our departure would have no more impact than our arrival. As we took the steep descent from the village, there was a sudden roar behind us and a school bus, carrying half a dozen blank-faced children, overtook us on a hairpin bend. We slid to a stop, inches from the parapet wall separating us from oblivion.

---

1 Most beautiful villages (French tourist classification)
2 Book Feast

With shaking legs, we got out of the car to gulp some cold mountain air. Across the valley, I'm sure I heard the sound of duelling banjos. This is a true story, dear readers.

We shall return in the spring. Preferably on a guided tour.

Gaz and I have now received our Senior Citizens Railcard. We have booked our first rail journey to Marseille next week.

12

La vie en rose

February 2018

No matter how beautiful the place where I live, my joy or my despair is made by the people I'm with. It was ever thus.

We were fortunate to have friends already here. Bassie has always been generous with her friends, wanting them to know one another. Making social connections has dragged me out of my homesickness and into the 'doing stuff' that is at the heart of the expat community.

Being a part of it has given me a small insight into the difficulties of immigrants who come to our own country. I'm seeing behind the stereotype of both immigrant and expat. When you live in a country with a strange language and strange customs, it is natural to cling to the familiar and many Brits still long for their baked beans and Marmite. Almost all make an effort to speak the language, but that foreignness never goes away. Many Brits say that they have tried hard to form friendships with local people, to no avail. One socially adept Francophile who has lived here for twenty-five years told me he numbered only four French amongst his friends. Is it that old saw that humour and poetry do not translate? Or do you need a hook, like a sport or a shared interest to break down cultural barriers? Obviously, the words 'family' and 'familiar' have the same root. Perhaps incomers cleave to their own language-speakers in order to form replacement families? I am pondering on these imponderables as I give a cheery wave to our neighbours. We are trying really hard with our merry smiles and waves and will, I am sure, eventually make tentative conversation. And I'm certainly going to find the French for, 'Will you stop your bloody dog from barking all day long?'

In the meantime I am revelling in meeting the English-speaking ladies of Languedoc. My first introduction was at a venue close to here, Chateau St. Pierre de Serjac. The event was billed as a tapas and jazz evening but in fact the music was provided by two Catalan gypsy guitarists who were joined every so often by a young female singer from the table next to ours. Soon her companions were dancing and we, the observers, were transported to a northern Spanish gypsy campfire. As our table of ten Brits loudly showed our appreciation, I looked around at my companions and anticipated, with some pleasure, the part they might play in our adventure.

In appreciation of our support, this dark-haired young woman stood at the end of our table and sang, hand on brow, a highly emotional rendition of *La Vie en Rose*. Life seen through rosé-tinted wine glasses seems fine by me!

Only two days later, we joined some of those we had already

47

met and some fascinating others for a Sunday roast: two courses, wine and coffee for €22 a head. The venue was Domaine L'Aise in St. Pargoire, twenty minutes from home. Once again, kind new friends, Richard and Jill, transported us there. This beautiful, very old home, high in the hills, has amazing views. It is owned and run by Karen and Mike as a *chambres d'hôtes*[1] so their summer lives are very busy with guests. In the winter they host these occasional lunches. Fourteen of us sat down to eat traditional British fare. The conversation flowed over an amazing variety of subjects, and there was laughter and *bonhomie*[2]. As we retired for coffee and *pastis*[3] to a long table in the warmth of a sunny, January afternoon, I understood that here was part of what I had been missing.

I have joined Ladies in Languedoc, a three thousand strong internet-based support group for English speaking women in France. They offer help and information on any subject under the sun, from schools to finding a cobbler, and everything in between. They organise outings too. All this to help combat the possible loneliness of the stranger in a strange land. It has proved to be a lifeline for many of its members. I have been invited to join Ladies in Pézenas, a much smaller and more social group, as well as Books, Wine and Chips. I start my creative writing classes in March. Gaz and I continue our conversation classes with a different and equally lovely group. Goodness, come the summer, I shall have no time to sunbathe.

Just a footnote really, and despite promises not to mention it, while out yesterday, the second week in February, we counted eleven Santas still struggling over balconies with their still laden though rather grubby sacks, and glimpsed in one house a fully lit and laden Christmas tree. Just saying.

---

1 Bed and breakfast
2 Good nature, camaraderie
3 Aniseed liqueur

13

Whoever doesn't jump is not from Marseille (French football song)

February 2018

The train strike was cancelled so, only an hour late, we boarded our train to Marseille. Gaz had read somewhere that the French always take a picnic on board so he made big rolls and added a bottle of Picpoul and despite my reservations regarding etiquette, we excitedly unpacked our goodies as we sped through lovely French countryside. Farms and flamingoes, vineyards and freight yards whizzed by.

'Glasses?' I enquired.

'Forgot,' he replied.

Despite my embarrassment we sipped daintily from the bottle. Classy or what?

Marseille station is a thing of ultra-modern beauty. They have even copied the St. Pancras open piano which was being effortlessly played by a young Frenchman. Outside, Gary consulted Miles Satnav on his phone to locate our town centre hotel. Yes, that same Miles who leads us into perilous situations and has the worst French accent in the world. Now, either Miles has taken against us because of all the times we have shouted, 'Shut the (swear word) up. How can we return to the bloody route if we don't know where the bloody route is?' or some malicious person has slipped him an internet version of a psychotic drug. Either way, he's being weird.

'This way, darling,' says Gazzie merrily.

We set off down a perpendicular cobbled road, our cute little cases clippity-clopping behind us . . . into the jaws of hell.

I'm not saying it was a rough neighbourhood but I feared for my very fillings. Even the sun was a luxury not to be afforded amongst the mountains of debris that spilled from every opening. Men sat in groups on the ground smoking and throwing dice and we jumped three feet off the ground when one said, 'Bonjour. Ça va? Morning! How are you?'

Every conceivable surface was covered in graffiti. I have never seen such a proliferation of this questionable art. Walls, doors, windows, shopfronts, cars all covered. Animals too, I suspect. Through chattering teeth I said to Gaz, 'Don't stand still or you'll find a Banksy on your bottom.'

When thinking about this later I was a bit sorry we hadn't stopped. I thought, 'Mmm. Banksy on bottom. Remove Banksy with several layers of bottom. Sell Banksy and keep bottom reduction.' A silver lining can be found in most things.

Finally we saw light filtering through the darkness and came out onto a sunny street. Totally un-graffitied people sat in groups chatting in Arabic, drinking coffee the colour of tar and treating their Arabic-speaking friends like family.

Unbelievably, like a man seeking advice from someone who has just directed him into a burning building, Gazzie once again sought advice from Rat Face (worst French accent, etc.).

'Straight up here, darling,' he said, a little less gaily than last time.

Up was right. You needed a ladder to walk up this road.

'Only another five minutes,' he said, soothingly.

An hour later, while I was strapping on an oxygen cylinder and adjusting a face mask, he said, 'I think Miles Satnav told us wrong.'

We turned and made our way back down the road. My face was set in a rictus of pain caused by a two hour walk on arthritic joints. We had passed our hotel twice without Miles S. once saying, 'And your destination is on your left.' When we finally found it without his help, we checked in, fell on the bed and slept.

On waking, we resolved to avoid 'the poorer places where the ragged people go', as young Paul Simon said, and so found ourselves – no, you are absolutely not going to believe it but actually Miles Satnav found us – in an area, just by the Metro, of sullen streets and silent strangers. By this time though, hunger made us immune to danger and in this, the second largest city of France, home of the *bouillabaisse*[1], we had a delicious Indian meal, but without poppadoms.

'French won't eat them,' the waiter told us. What?

Like mornings in all the best stories, our morrow dawned blue and gold. The hotel was ideally placed in the shopping area and only minutes from the old port where we sat and ate our omelettes in the hundred-year-old restaurant, La Samaritaine. We were transfixed by Norman Foster's masterpiece *Miroir Ombrière*[2], built to shade visitors to the port and to reflect the lives of those who visited it. Being an artist, I bet he didn't think of the poor souls who have to clean it. Several contortionists were attempting to do so as we watched.

---

1 Provençale fish stew
2 Literally, 'mirror shade'

As we try to do, whenever visiting a new town, we took the Big Bus Tour and were driven right up to Notre Dame de la Garde which stands high above the town, via a hair-raising route through narrow urban streets where we bullied small cars out of our way. We held our breath as the bus teetered over the rocks above the Frioul archipelago and we sighed with relief as it dropped down to drive along the elegant corniche of the seafront, past the town's diverse architecture and back to the old port. Too full and too frozen to stop for the bouillabaisse being served at most of the portside restaurants, we returned to the hotel to thaw.

In France, retail shops are allowed sales only for six weeks from mid-January and so we felt it our duty to support the local economy and tried our best to buy, but apart from a pair of pink patent leather brogues that called to me, even the sale prices were beyond our budget.

It was our last evening. Gazzie did his navigation without Rat Face and found a delightful bistro in the Opéra region, just two blocks back from the port. Named l'Horloge, it was narrow with one line of tables, giving close access to the neighbour's food, and their dogs, should you be so inclined. The staff, all youngsters, were absolutely delightful with huge smiles and a nothing-too-much-trouble attitude. We were busy using Google Translate to decipher the menu when, to the amusement of our close neighbours, the nice waiter pointed out there was an English translation beneath the French.

Gazzie had the octopus which he pronounced delicious and I had a gourmet cottage pie with pulled beef cheek and almonds. Then we shared a plate of *fromage*, cheese, as yummy as a very yummy thing, and a *pichet*[3] of quaffable dry white wine. All this for a princely thirty euros a head and more people-watching and story-making than your heart could desire.

---

3 Glass jug of wine, usually a half-litre

The lights of the port lit our way home. Perfect.

Despite security alerts at the station, and a thirty minute delay, the journey home was very pleasant. And there was our foster mum, Bassie, waiting for us in an illegal parking area, ready to take us to our foster home in Roujan.

We light the fire. Gaz turns on the rugby. I groan. We are home.

14

Putting on the style

February 2018

Having carried his golf clubs with us from England, we felt it imperative that Gary should use them. Early research indicated that membership in the Béziers Golf Club for a little over ten months would be €1800. Much as I wanted him to play, this was way beyond our budget and we agreed it wasn't feasible.

A bit more research found a nine hole course, costing half as much. Off we went to view it on a sunny day in January. It is a pretty course, long and narrow and following the path of a river. A newly built clubhouse offered such a good standard of food and drink that it was open to the public. Any worries about dress code were quickly allayed when we watched a young man teeing off in jeans and leather jacket with a Gauloise stuck firmly between his teeth.

After his first game, Gaz seemed happy enough, but he had lost six balls: four in the river and two under one of the many coypu who, with the odd duck or two, wander around the course. Gary pretends they are his golfing buddies since he has not yet had the confidence to chat to other golfers, despite the fact that most golfing terms have strong roots in English: *les green fees, le pitching et le putting*, and so on. I hope he will get over that shyness. A bit lonely 'til then. Coypu and duck aren't big on conversation.

The course is on the outskirts of Lamalou-les-Bains, a very pretty town where this golf widow looks forward to many a happy hour in the ancient spa, rolled in mud or whatever they did before essential oils came along while, on the golf course, Gaz is holing in one.

Off the golf course, our diaries were filling up with visits from friends from the UK which gave us the excuse to visit new places and revisit favourites. I began to feel like a Norman Foster groupie when we drove to the Massif Central to see his viaduct at Millau. Once again the weather gods favoured us because, like a conjuror revealing his finest trick, the curtain of mist lifted to reveal an edifice both strong and delicate and most worthy of its iconic status. Why is it that a bit of beauty always makes me hungry? Declining the guided tour of the caves in which the Roquefort cheese is kept, we decided we'd rather taste it in the town that gave the cheese its name. It's surprising how many dishes you can add Roquefort to. We tried quite a few.

Returning our friends to their departure airport in Carcassonne allowed us to have a lightning tour of this ancient town, one of the most visited in the south of France. There wasn't enough time, but we shall definitely return.

So, another goodbye. Another little airport. Another afterthought: as I got into Mistress R. Soul for the homeward journey, a gust of wind grabbed hold of my long scarf and then banged the door. Shut. Isadora Duncan-style. My face made intimate contact with the window. I tried to rescue my scarf but it was stuck fast around the lock. The door would neither open nor close. Freed from my end of the scarf, I spent the journey hanging onto the door in case a bump suddenly dislodged the scarf and the door flew open with me fast behind.

That car hates me.

15

And what will the robin do then, poor thing?

March 2018

We sunbathed in January and now, as we welcome the month of March, in solidarity with our comrades in the UK, we have whiteout. Snow is unusual here and has fallen only once in the last four years when our neighbours' teenage children saw it for the first time.

We have watched youngsters and animals today, seeing, feeling and tasting snow. Their joy was contagious, but not enough to draw us outside.

The downside of an area which sees hardly any snow is that most drivers are not used to the conditions. People are seeking assistance all over Languedoc, either because they have become stuck in their cars or, worse, they have had accidents. The Ladies in Languedoc Facebook page has been inundated with cries for help and offers of support. Social networking at its best.

However, priorities are different here. As we stood indoors watching, me with my Guides First Aider badge clasped in my hand and Gazzie in his Ambulance Man uniform (my favourite, second only to the Fireman one), our neighbour opposite climbed onto his flat roof to try to brush off the snow as it fell.

. . . and yesterday, yes yesterday, Gazzie was sunbathing. (You know about that but it's getting worse, my friends. Remember when he stripped off when someone switched on a light? Well, yesterday, a friend wandered round with a lighted cigarette and he was disrobed, sun creamed and on the newly purchased sunlounger before I could say, 'There's snow forecast.')

Where was I? Oh yes. Terday.

'If winter comes, can spring be far behind?' said ol' Willie Shakespeare. Well, they do things differently here, sir. Spring skips onto the scene followed by an Arctic permafrost.

16

Le centre du monde (Salvador Dalí on Perpignan)

March 2018

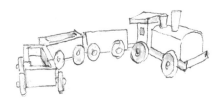

It has been the worst winter for forty years, and aspersions are being cast on the coincidence of this phenomenon with our arrival.

However, on Saturday, sun was forecast and Gaz was offering me various options for activities on this warm and sunny day. We had planned to visit the Abrivado at Le Grau-du-Roi, a bull running festival which demonstrates the skills of the horsemen and the bravery of young men against agile, long-horned Camargue bulls. It is not a blood sport and no blood is spilt, rather a tradition amongst the *gitans* of the Camargue and, so we are told, a spectacle not to be missed. However, we were destined for disappointment because the event was postponed due to the adverse weather. So, not *that* brave, those young men. With Bassie and Hugh (the friends who started this whole adventure) we decided instead to visit Perpignan, new to us all.

Nice to have a bit of culture from time to time. Hugh drove, so a lovely break for Gazzie.

Amazingly, even though Perpignan is only seventy miles from where we live, there was no snow, but as we drove towards the town, the Pyrenees, rising before us, were completely white.

There are more stunning cities than you can shake a stick at around here. Perpignan takes some beating though. Home, years ago, to the Kings of Majorca, there is a strong Catalan influence throughout the city and amongst the people. That's all the historical education I'm giving you.

We were in shirt sleeves. Where do we get these sayings? Why would anyone go naked except for the sleeves of a shirt? We parked easily and walked into brilliant sunshine. We savoured the view as we sipped our coffee and shared our croissants.

After a wander through the old town, looking longingly into shop windows of high fashion and even higher prices, we had lunch in the town square where residents and visitors came together for a good lunch under blue skies.

We are still very new to the French language of course, and often have to check things on Google Translate. So, for your information, if you see on a menu, *tomette de brebis*, the dish you can look forward to is 'a floor tile of ewe'.

Afterwards, we made our way through ancient streets to the stop for the little tourist train.

The Basilique-Cathédrale de Saint Jean-Baptiste de Perpignan looks almost modern from the outside, but the inside filled us with wonder and reverence. Whilst neither of us is conventionally religious, we were moved to tears by the beauty of the building. I was right to leave my cynicism on the doorstep and to go inside ready to embrace whatever we found.

And so to the relative normality of the Little Train.

Gazzie and I were transported right back to the Romney, Hythe and Dymchurch Railway where we had many, many happy times with our grandson over the course of a couple of years, feeding his obsession with Thomas the Tank Engine. We said, in unison, as we boarded the train:

'Thomas the Engine is blue. Percy has a big funnel.'

'Here comes the Fat Controller.' That's what I said to my grandson whenever grandpa Gary appeared. Ah, how hilarious we were. Happy days!

Still, I digress.

The tour was fascinating. We bib bibbed and toot tooted through the narrow streets where the shops were so close we could have shoplifted. The train wouldn't have made much of a getaway vehicle though. We made our way higher and higher and were asked to put away our cameras when we trundled through the Gypsy Quarter. Catalan Gypsies (*Gitans*, remember?) are a valued part of the community here. There were maybe a hundred men, women and children in the square, talking, playing, being. They were mostly dressed in black but there was a friendly, happy atmosphere and certainly an air of self-parody from the young man who shouted, 'Don't stop or I'll have your tyres off.' In Catalan, naturally, but I worked it out from his gestures. I think.

Every time the tourist information tape stopped, we had a jolly song about Perpignan which soon we were all singing along to. It seemed to have more to do with a German oompah band than anything French but nonetheless, we bounced and swayed in a jolly touristy way.

Back in the town we stopped in Tiger to buy silly glasses and laugh and laugh. No young children, no Fat Controller, just four not-young adults 'acting more like children than children'. We had felt like kings, enjoying the beneficence that was our due and like paupers who had savoured every crumb. Sometimes, that's how a day goes.

17

A many splendored thing

March 2018

This morning, for the first time since arriving in France in December, and because hot weather was forecast, I decided to sit in the garden and catch up on my blog. I tickled my memory bank, applied sun oil and had my finger poised over my phone, for it is on there that I do my writing, when I became aware that, close by, rehearsals appeared to be in progress for a performance of *The Hound of the Baskervilles* – the un-musical! Every damned dog in Languedoc seemed to have a part and each one barked or howled in a different key. I went inside until rehearsals were over, despite rather falling in love with one of the soloists. It was later, on recounting the incident that I found that no such un-musical was planned, but that this was a daily occurrence. At least twice a day, the *Mairie*[1] uses the public address system to alert villagers to important events of the day, such as the imminent arrival of the shellfish van from Bouzigues. They start each broadcast with ding dongs (of the *Hi-de-Hi!* variety) followed by 'Allo, Allo.' This custom has been followed for many, many years and is the derivation of the name of the British television series. The ding dongs are in an exact register to cause the local hounds to howl and bark.

Since the snow went, the skies have mostly been blue and our days continue to be filled with wonder at new surroundings and people. I have continued to meet amazing women: artists, ceramicists, writers, housewives, many of whom have decided that, with or without partners, they will make a life in this part of France. Despite my misgivings earlier, that one cannot make friends with the local people, I met a British couple who have achieved exactly that and count many French people in their friendship group. It seems too that when friendships are made here, they are fed, watered and regularly maintained. I like that.

Recently I met such a group of women in a scruffy little café with lovely food, in the village of Paulhan. We ate outside in the middle of February. We have been in France for three months and despite periods of homesickness I am also experiencing periods of deep contentment and, yes, belonging. But, dear readers, as we all know, 'there's no friends like old friends.' And Lordy, I've got some old friends. Ho, ho, ho.

We anticipated the arrival of said old friends with a pleasure born of the knowledge that they would love this area. But, as I previously hinted, Gaz and I are not the most confident cooks on earth and this couple are . . . whisper it on the wind . . . vegetarian. Whilst France has moved some way towards encompassing meatless eaters, we had been advised to check with restaurants before booking. So I did. After giving the

1 Mayor's office. Town hall

63

restaurant the news, the manager asked whether our friends ate eggs or fish. I'm sure I detected a French '*pffff*' at the news that they did not. We therefore set off for Le Pré St. Jean, in Pézenas, with a few concerns. There was a crowd of people in the vicinity of the restaurant. 'Here to see if vegetarians really have two heads,' muttered our friend, John. Obviously disappointed, they moved speedily away as a rumour broke that, in the next town, a lone vegan had been spotted. Our restaurant had gone into overdrive and produced a meal for our friends the like of which they had seldom seen. They even had their own version of *amuse-bouche*. We were mightily impressed.

We revisited Sète with Nicki and John. I have not grown to like this town. It should be pretty, set as it is on the Étang de Thau and with the canal running through the centre, but somehow it is too busy, and too grubby. We returned to Lamalou where Gazzie and John played golf and Nicki jumped up and down with excitement at seeing the coypu, and frightened them off. We took sustenance outside the Club House, got sunburnt, Gaz got food poisoning, and we all went home.

Actually we think Gaz's illness started the night before, after eating oysters. It took a couple of days for the food police to identify a norovirus in oysters from the Étang, at which point all sales were forbidden. Gary was unlucky.

Waving goodbye to our friends at Béziers train station, we set off back home a little disconsolately since all that was waiting for us was a soggy lettuce and the telly. Now I love TV at home, but trying to watch it here is like using the old Crystal Set or Cat's Whisker radio kit. Wires trail from TV to iPad, from iPad to God knows where and a whole new language is required to turn the bloody thing on.

'Oh, no, the VPN knows we're in France!'

'What's that, the French Secret Service?'

'Oh no! It's buffering.'

'No signal.'

All before we get a programme.

The following day was a big rugby thingy. France v England. Gary, feeling stronger now, lined up his red wine bottles and packets of Hula Hoops, and with the excitement of a child going to his first picnic, set off to a friend's house to do a manly television watch which meant they could swear a bit since no ladies would be present. I thought.

He came through the door some four hours later and when I asked the score (good wife) he made a strange signal with his hand which I thought meant he was about to throw up again. Then the front door burst open. My heart leapt to my mouth and I screamed like a banshee until I saw it was my daughter and her friend, Georgia, here to spend Mother's Day with us. I think I went slightly mad, crying and laughing and kissing and hugging . . . and there was Gazzie, standing in the corner smiling, having given up his precious rugby to collect the girls and please the people he loves most. That man deserves . . . well, to watch his rugby in peace. Which he did on the Cat's Whisker television after us gals had fallen tipsily into bed.

We are back in the UK in two weeks' time for various celebrations. I have no idea, at this moment, how I'm going to feel.

18

Jazz

March 2018

She could never have imagined
not that little girl
her brown eyes level with the kitchen table
the grandma saying 'There is no Christmas'
That little girl
many years on
sitting with someone who loves her
watching a jazz quartet
in an ancient beamed room, lit by candles
in a small village in Southern France
That little girl, there
Then more than seventy Christmases
wrapped themselves around her
and gifts of peace and contentment

and simple joy
fell like leaves
into the soul
of that little girl.

19

Fever? Yeah I burn forsooth

April 2018

You may remember, dear and faithful readers, that as I set off for my homeland I said I had no idea how I would feel. I could not have imagined I would feel thus:

– being run over by a Sherman tank which then reversed

– having my head in a vice operated by the Incredible Hulk

– having my legs removed, simmered in aspic and then sewn back on by a blind juggler (nice try though)

– my lungs housing two Tasmanian Devils sometimes loudly purring, other times trying to claw their way up through to my throat.

Well, that is a close proximity to how I felt for eight of the eleven days I was away.

Now, I enjoy a good illness along with the next hypochondriac but never, never, have I felt so ill in all my life. And so, whilst we managed the first weekend's round of wonderful parties, I spent the rest of the time in a friend's bed. The doc diagnosed flu, the first of my life, said I was highly contagious, so I had to save humanity by keeping away from it. A trick a few politicians could learn!

The first weekend started with a family lunch at my daughter's club which was closing the following day. I sat there surrounded by the people who are my very life's blood, smiling inanely. Gaz and I have spent so many happy times there since before the grandchildren, now in their twenties, were born: christenings, weddings, the best New Year's Eve parties in town. And watched the children mature as their parties became less and less mature. A real reason to celebrate and remember all the fun times. And now the club is becoming a school again, which is what it used to be. Fitting. And hopefully as much fun.

At the party the next evening I saw people I hadn't seen for ages. It all became very emotional. But what separates human kind from other kinds? Emotion. I kissed, I cuddled, I licked, I stroked. I started a flu pandemic.

Tears were shed, forming raging torrents along the streets as we prepared to leave. Friends gathered to offer a totally un-melodic, but nonetheless just recognisable rendition of, 'So long, Farewell, Auf Wiedersehen, Goodbye.' Gary and I slished and sloshed our way back to our hotel.

And then I slipped into a world of delirium. We'd managed visits to Gary's mum and dad and were at the home of friends in Gravesend. The coughing started, fortunately waking me from dreams of terrible, red-eyed beasts, snakes in my hair, village people between my toes (no, not those Village People), Boris Johnson as Foreign Secretary. Terrible, terrible visions. We managed to drag ourselves to our beloved Whitstable where our one-night stay with Jenny and Mark turned into five. Gary made merry little forays to friends' houses, saying, as he entered, 'Oh, silly me, I haven't taken off my doctor's uniform. It's been hell looking after her, pure hell. My poor beloved.' I languished in

69

sweat-soaked sheets with my demons, touching neither food nor wine. I think that was part of the fever – Prosecco-withdrawal symptoms. I couldn't read, watch TV, or speak. Every so often Gary came in and squeezed a few drops of water onto my parched lips from a flannel. Like they do in films. I have a feeling, though, it's a clean one in the films whereas my water had the distinct taste of Dove Pure.

Gary played golf on his old Whitstable course. He met old golfing buddies, went to the pub with Jenny and Mark and I could hear their gay laughter along the corridor as I lay on my sodden sheets with a bit of old flannel hanging out of my mouth.

I missed a book club meeting with my gorgeous bookworms and worse, missed seeing Viv's ninety-nine-year-old mother! Too dangerous the doc said. For me. Oh, and a hastily reconvened gathering of the Silly Games Players. I might have understood some of the games without copious amounts of Prosecco. Hell and damnation and many, many buggerrrrrrs.

There was one last reason for us to go home: Maz's 70th birthday party.

On Saturday morning my energy level had dropped to zero. Opening my eyelids had been achieved with the aid of a mini hydraulic lift. I had to be spoon fed water: 'I'm not gonna make it' . . . (no, not die . . . to the party). I went for a bath at noon and crawled out at four. Then three hours to dress.

'Let's go parteee!'

With the help of a partially-willing friend, I made it down the three million steps to Maz's. I suddenly felt rather shy about going in, as if the illness had stripped me not just of my energy but all the other things needed by the seasoned party animal. There was a whoosh as the door opened and out poured warmth and laughter and smiling faces and open hands.

'Jan and Gazzie!' they seemed to say. 'You're home. Come on in and be loved.'

And so we did. And so we were.

The journey back to France wasn't easy, but we made it. I'm still coughing like a very coughy thing but the fever has gone.

20

The hills are alive

April 2018

L'été[1] has indeed arrived in our village but in my bedroom the weather feels tropical as my temperature continues to rise and my eyelids, too heavy to lift, stay closed, off and on, for four days. French doctors have been called, more drugs administered, and gradually over ten days, I've almost returned to normal though often weary to my very bones. My daughter, Sara, and her husband, SuperBri, have been staying and so outings continued. I was carefully ladled in and out of cars and slept through some of the most amazing scenery in Europe.

After going on long, energetic walks to Neffiès and Gabian, the young ones agreed to Gazzie's offer of a chauffeured research day to check out venues for their next sporting adventure. So off we went to Roquebrun – remember, dear readers, we went there in January – and it was even more beautiful in warm,

---

1 Summer

bright sunshine. They looked in excitement and anticipation at the swollen river while I fretted over my swollen ankles, caused by that damned W thing after so long abed. The possibility of kayaking here though was nil. The river was in spate and water thundered and gushed dramatically over the rocks after exceptionally heavy rain. Just another aside here, I do sometimes wonder whether my children were switched at birth. Thinking on, there was a woman, well, more a suggestion of a woman really, in the maternity ward, who jumped out of bed half an hour after giving birth and did a five-minute warm-up before doing five circuits of the ward. Her baby was sitting in the cot reading *This Sporting Life*. My baby lay next to me trying to summon up the energy to purse its lips to feed while I fondly whispered, 'In your own time, Tiger.'

We decided to drive further into the mountains. Our lifestyle gurus, having found no activities and no refreshment (the pursuit of which was another favourite sport), were beginning to look longingly at the strangely brown and scraggy sheep on the strangely brown and scraggy hillside (could have been a mirage, I suppose), so we consulted maps and decided to make for the village of Maroul, ten minutes' away, where there seemed to be a hostelry. We phoned ahead.

'*Oui*,' said Madame. '*Nous avons une table pour vous.*' Yes, we have a table for you.

The ten minutes must have been as Concorde flew, for it took considerably longer, not that it mattered as we climbed higher and higher through pine forests, punctuated with little waterfalls tumbling down to the road and cherry trees, hardly able to hold their white blossom. A tiny village of maybe fifty houses finally came into view.

There was a Tyrolean feel to the place and I half-expected Julie Andrews to appear with blonde, bent-up pigtails, singing *'High on a hill was a lonely goatherd'*. We climbed up to the

73

auberge, past little houses in streets identified by their names handwritten on slate, and were very warmly welcomed by Madame. The *menu du jour*[2] was twenty-three euros and included Roquefort tart, stuffed leg of guinea fowl and strawberries three ways. A *pichet* of house wine was better than anything we had yet tasted in France. We were the only guests. We felt chosen. We felt privileged. We had found our very own bit of heaven.

The following day we all went to Béziers. Still no kayaking. No, dear readers, not for me. Remember what I said about the wetsuit? The rivers were still too swollen. But we found a pretty part of Béziers that we had not previously discovered.

As we were close by, we visited Les Neufs Écluses de Fonséranes, the third most visited tourist attraction in Languedoc after Carcassonne and the Pont du Gard. The staircase locks here consist of eight ovoid lock chambers which raise boats to twenty-one metres, in the past a very important part of the Canal du Midi but now used mostly for tourist traffic.

More adventures included a visit to Chez Paul in Pézenas where all courses are served together on one slab of slate. It works. Don't ask me how. And we returned to Chateau St Pierre de Serjac where lunch took five hours. Our exhausted little group got together for a last evening before the young ones set out on the next leg of their European tour.

This was never going to be easy for me, still weak, waving goodbye to our lovely girl and her man, not knowing when we would see them again. It was fortuitous that we four were invited to friends for *apéro*. Now I'm not sure if this is a French thing or a Languedoc thing or even an expat thing, but it is rather like the old UK cocktail party. Arrive at 6.30 pm, drink and eat nibbles, and leave at about 8.30 pm. Not something I look forward to because I'm not sure of the rules. But we were treated

---

2 Menu of the day

royally to wine and Persian food, warmth and laughter, making that last evening very special.

And so more goodbyes, more tears, both happy and sad. Gaz and I walked back in the house, raced upstairs, and started making everything clean and comfortable for the next visitors. And that complete rest I was supposed to be having? Time for that when I get old.

21

Another oeuf-ful day

May 2018

One thing I didn't expect was that I'd be measuring the seasons by the countryside. I have never been, and suspect never will be, a country gal, but the lives of the villages are determined by the seasons and particularly by the seasons of the vine. In winter, the vine trunks squat like little black skeletons right across the landscape. Stark and stumpy, it is almost impossible to believe that there is life in those dark veins. And yet by February or March a lime, almost translucent, green, starts to break through in vineyards everywhere. For we are surrounded by vineyards and they have dictated the lives of the people of this area for thousands of years. At one time, virtually the whole community was involved in some way or another, working for the separate *domaines* or wine growing dynasties. Now in May, close inspection reveals tiny grapes forming with the *vignerons*[1] checking the progress of their charges on a daily basis.

A lot of the *domaines* have returned to their independent status after the popularity of the massive co-operatives waned amid accusations of inferior quality. Some of the huge buildings stand empty, falling into disrepair. But with lessons learnt, smaller wine growers are again producing co-operative wine. Here, the most popular grape is Picpoul. We first tasted this crisp white wine at the Goods Shed in Canterbury; now we watch it growing. It gives us a sense of almost parental pride.

So, we were excited to be going to our first *dégustation*[2] to taste the rosé wine from the Sarabande *domaine*. It is a tiny *domaine* owned and run by Isla from Ireland and Paul from Australia. They have two young children; they grow the vines, and do the weeding, tending and picking, before producing delightful reds and rosés. At first, I declined a glass of rosé, on the basis that I didn't like it.

'I know you will love it,' Paul said, and I did.

I had to keep on trying but after a fair test of three glasses I agreed. Loverly. And dry as a bone. Technical term, unknown except among us wine quaficionados.

In their spare time, Isla and Paul make Sarabande gin which is rated highly enough to be sold to other countries. And they run different events around their year-long wine tastings. AND they never stop smiling.

We attend everything. If someone is inspecting a drain in the next village, we'll be there. At home, I wouldn't stir past the front door for less than a Michelin-starred meal and free champagne. OK, some of you know me so I must be honest – for a free meal and a bottle of Prosecco. Add in my renowned

---

1 Wine growers

2 a tasting session

fear of anything that isn't an actual human being, i.e. anything that goes under the generic description of *animal,* then dear readers, you would know the likelihood of seeing me in a field, at the end of nowhere, with a load of chickens was virtually nil.

So, Gazzie said, 'Would you like to come to see Brian the Egg Man and the chickens that produce your lovely morning eggs?'

'No.'

'But it's an idyllic spot in the country with chairs you can sit on and everything.'

'No.'

'Take you out for lunch after. With wine and stuff.'

'Can I stay in the car?'

'Yes, but you'll want to get out.'

I need to digress for a moment, but bear with me because it is relevant. Ever at the forefront of my mind, whatever the occasion, is what to wear, so in the absence of appropriate footwear such as Wellington boots, I had put on my black patent-leather thigh-high, four-inch heels, Jimmy Chews. OK, I was fooled. I should have guessed that the genuine article would have cost in excess of five hundred pounds not the twenty pounds I paid and been spelt correctly. Anyway, it was the only vaguely suitable footwear I had.

Then we drove to some godforsaken place, up dirt tracks, and had to walk, yes walk, for miles to an opening in a hedge where Brian sat with about eighty chickens. Honestly? The noise and the smell were horrendous. Yet the other three adults cooed and clucked and stroked the beaky things. I admitted – I am not a total philistine – that some of the iridescent feathers were pretty, but when Brian said, 'Jan, do you want to hold this egg? It's straight from the hen,' I shuddered and politely replied, 'No thank you dear, let it cool down, put it in a nice grey box with five others and I'll pretend it came from a supermarket.'

One interesting thing occurred to me though. The chickens were eating the vine leaves and presumably they would eat the grapes when they came. A bit of fermentation and I could have wine-infused eggs for breakfast. I think it could catch on.

The other three finally gave in and tore themselves away. I was pleased to get back to the car until a nasal-passage-scorching, eye-watering odour told me that our driver had taken the opportunity to bring three tonnes of chicken poo back for his garden. Ah, the joys of country life.

We were invited to afternoon tea with Brian's sister Sharon in her house in Roujan. It is an enormous three-storey conversion project. The gardens have been done, the pool installed and an amazing, enormous kitchen finished. The whole of the top floor and roof are yet to be rebuilt and, unfortunately, some of the work already undertaken is seriously sub-standard. Sharon seems philosophical about it all, but then she lost her farm, her home and most of her possessions to the Mugabe pogroms in her native home of Zimbabwe. After the unimaginable horrors of her last years there, I suspect a leaking roof is small fry. She is a brave, bright, intelligent woman and I hope we shall become friends. Despite . . . the three dogs, two cats and the chicken sanatorium housing chickens at every stage from incubator to old age. What is it with people and animals here?

To round off this treatise on wine, I must add that Sharon is a wine importer, selling South African wine to newish markets such as China. However, now that she lives in France and has a French partner, they hope to produce wine for their own label. She gave Gary a whole bottle of Rhône wine which he had difficulty describing: 'Oh, oh, it's . . . oh.' An adjectivally challenged man, our Gaz, who later found out that the wine was rated in the top two percent of Rhône wines.

I, on the other hand, received only one glass of a nice white. I'll give her one more chance to be my friend. Just one.

22

Friendly faces, familiar places

May 2018

The countryside is singing with wildflowers of every kind and the garden of our little home is awash with colour. Not many French homes seem to have flower gardens, perhaps because of the extremely hot summers that we have been warned about, but not so far experienced.

We've been to the local airports to collect and return visitors so often that people think we work there. Fortunately, Gary also loves a pilot's uniform! We said yet another teary farewell yesterday to friends from Whitstable who, unbeknownst to us, had a five and half hour delay while 'spare parts' were awaited from across the globe to glue the plane together. God protect us from Mr Ryanair!

One of the challenges of entertaining visitors is that we return to places we've already been. So when asked if we get bored with showing off our lovely countryside, the answer is, 'Not so far.' But it could happen. Anyway, friends are all different and see things from their own perspectives. Visiting the Canal du Midi with Mandy and John opened our eyes to new aspects of this interesting waterway. Like: 'Where would you join the canal if you were on your boat?' wondered Sailor Mandy. And we discovered where. In an apparently almost deserted part of the canal.

Gazzie obviously gets a bit bored with all the pastoral and watery idylls and decides to scare the living bejeebers out of me by going up mountains. So whilst I was thoroughly enjoying the coffee and house-sized baguettes in Fraisse-sur-Agout, Gaz was wanting to go ever onwards and upwards, fantasising that he was Sherpa Tenzing on his way up Everest. I'm sure he threw a thick rope in the back of the car together with pitons, crampons and other climbing paraphernalia. Honestly, the man's only ever been on a day trip to the Lake District yet you'd think he'd equipped and taken part in an Everest expedition. We strapped on breathing apparatus and jumped back in the car. I didn't see much of the scenery because my head was in Mandy's lap.

'Gary, take this bloody car downwards this instant!' I screamed.

He ignored me and carried on to his destination which was a rather disappointing watery place called Lac du Laouzas. Not worth the climb in my humble opinion, but the others coloured themselves impressed in order to curry favour with the driver.

Revisiting Olargues in the pouring rain was a new experience. Cobbled, perpendicular streets, rain and flip-flops are not a great combination but we found a welcoming café (just the one open in a back street) with hot coffee and sandwiches. Back in dear Mistress R. Soul, her boot jangling with climbing aids, we ooh-d and ahh-d through misty car windows at what I'm sure was gorgeous, if moisture laden, scenery.

Back home, Gazzie barbecued while our guests ate indoors, and I went to my first proper book club meeting; the previous one had been a 'social'. We discussed *Eleanor Oliphant is Completely Fine* whilst drinking rosé wine and eating chips and mayonnaise! The only way to do it.

And then *Time To Say Goodbye* (cue Andrea Bocelli and Sarah Brightman). These goodbyes are doin' my head in! (cue Joe Brown and the Bruvvers).

Normal living in Languedoc is now rolling nicely for Gazzie and me with our golf, our clubs and other groups. I love meeting people and hearing how they came to live in this area. And my weeks speed by in pleasant busyness. I am looking forward, not back, and feeling hopeful.

23

Into each life a little rain must fall

May 2018

I have been in danger, latterly at least, of presenting our lives as a hedonistic idyll. I've even photographed meals for God's sake! My intention was always to tell it how it is and not give the impression of never-ending outings, with a never-ending procession of visitors and never-ending jollity. Whilst it would be boring for you to read about them, we do have periods without guests, when we stay at home, do washing and ironing and shop for food. I still have days of terrible homesickness and a physical ache for my family and friends. It ain't all beer and skittles. Know what I'm saying?

It is such a day today and it's hot as Hades outside. So I'll tell you about, and remind myself of, some more of the lovely stuff.

There are delights even on our own doorstep. We found out about a wine tasting at the local village of Laurens where our friend, Ginny, lives. Not just sips of wine either, a five course taster menu with wine matched to each course, and a singer from the Montpellier Opera Company.

'Sounds like our sorta gig, Gaz,' said I.

As you know, my word is his command, so he booked.

On the afternoon of this much anticipated occasion, as we watched the rain tear up paving slabs and the wind scoop up small people and deposit them inconveniently distant from their homes . . .

'Remind me, why are we going to this event?' Gaz asked.

'Opera singer,' I said.

He nodded.

'Wine,' I said.

He made a strange wiggly sign with his hand. He does that a lot.

'Food,' I said, more quietly because despite my size, it is not one of my overriding interests.

Pouring more cold water on the event than lashed down outside, he intoned, 'Wine will come a thimbleful at a time and with at least two of the courses it will be red. Which you don't drink. Those two courses are pork and then duck, one of which you don't like and the other you would never let into the country, let alone your mouth.'

'Opera singer?' I said faintly.

'You might be alright there,' he said.

Well, dear friends, you know me. By the end of the evening I was drinking red wine like a red wine drinker facing a red wine drought. I even did a bit of begging for other people's dregs. I made several new friends and Gary met four new golfing buddies so he doesn't have to play with himself anymore. Result.

Despite my drink stealing, I went home sober, hungry and with the prospect of losing Gary to golf three or four times a week. The opera singer was . . . the brother of the *vigneron*. Who was, incidentally, a woman (please keep up – the *vigneron*, not the singer). Oh, and a thimbleful is hardly enough to savour and judge a wine. In my opinion.

An aside: the next book to read and discuss at my book club is *The Sober Diaries*. Honestly, I should enjoy that one. I feel as if I've been in training.

Since arriving in this land of foreignness, I feel as if we attend one event and wake up the following morning, rubbing our hands, saying, 'OK, what's next?' There always seems to be a 'next'. Quick email to Social Secretary up the road (we actually call her Sexy Soc Sec, but only because we like a bit of sibilance in the mornings). Scanning her social diary, which I do believe takes up two walls in her garage, she informs us that, among many other events, it is the weekend of the Pézenas Brocantes Festival or Antiques Fair.

'Well, old thing, shall we go to see some more old things?' Gazzie laughed nervously as I retrieved my well-thumbed copy of *Home Castration*.

We went, though, eventually.

So, in the old country, Antiques Fairs are usually held in huge fields where, due to inevitable summer rain, one tramps around up to one's knees in mud and spends half an hour in the beer tent before heading home, having paid a tenner each entrance fee. Here, it rarely rains in May and the stalls line the main thoroughfares of concrete and tarmac. Live music plays, *paella*[1] is cooked on open fires, nothing is under cover, nor needs to be. There is no charge for wandering amongst the stalls of very unusual antiques. Which, dear readers, is just as well. The prices

---

1 Spanish rice dish

are astronomical. Obviously age is priceless. Are you listening, Gary? Sarcastic so-and-so.

24

Rituals and rites of passage

May 2018

May has dawned. There is a frisson of excitement amongst our friends, a sense that everything is about to start. It is the beginning of the summer season when folk go out every night.

The herald for this sybaritic summer is the Frog Fair, *La Fête de Grenouille*. Now I am not a great fan of frogs, alive or fried, but this looked both French and interesting. Hundreds of visitors crowded into Saint-Geniès-de-Fontedit, another ancient little village where I cannot but admire the sense of community, the obvious wish to preserve the past and embrace the present. There was a carnival atmosphere with brass bands, drummers and, inevitably, the cooking of frogs. A huge barbecue, maybe eight feet long, was already alight with thousands of raw frog legs waiting in the sun. Long trestle tables and chairs were set out for the diners. Before long there were twenty queues, maybe fifteen deep of salivating customers wanting to eat these little chopped off finger-like things. I shuddered and joined the chip queue.

We're off on our travels again! Poor old Mistress R. Soul will be blowing a gasket if we don't rest her soon but there's so much to see and so little time.

Our friends Johnny and Maz have returned. They've come so often we've given them a French name, *Les Fromages,* The Cheeses. Gosh, we are so witty. Sometimes I almost laugh. They bought us gifts of flamingoes, blow up ones to hold our drinks when our dip pool is set up for the summer. If all goes well, the pool will be ready for revellers next week!

Les Fromages requested a *brocante* or Boot Fair and we found one for them at Bouzigues. (I know, faithful followers, we have been there several times, but *sans*[1] *brocante*). It was a beautiful setting with stalls set up along the seafront with friendly stallholders and a great variety of stuff. Money was spent by all. Our purchase finally proved that we have no idea of the worth or the aesthetic value of anything. We've hidden the lamp that cost us ten euros!

Gazzie and Johnny feasted on oysters and we women on chips, all washed down with a *pichet* of excellent white wine. Our host/ waitress at À La Voile Blanche was, we all agreed, the kindest, smiliest, nothing-too-much-troublest that we have ever met. Afterwards, to give our guests an extra treat, we decided to take the car ferry across the Petit-Rhône. Unluckily, there was a café serving beer at the terminal. The weak-willed men went to get one. The ferry tooted to go and in the time it took to pay for the blooming beers, the ferry went. Not willing to wait half an hour for the next one, we drove all the way back the way we came.

Next up was Saintes-Maries-de-la-Mer. When we visited in

---

1 Without

February, we saw a pretty little town with odd cone-shaped white houses and six people – gentlemen of a certain age, playing *boules* in the square. Our visit this time was five days before the festival day of Sainte Sara Kali, the Black Madonna, patron saint of gypsies, which attracts gypsies from all over Europe for the ceremony of taking her statue into the sea. I suppose even ancient plaster saints like a bit of a dip every so often. We expected to see some signs of preparation, but not this: car parks full of caravans and trailers and six thousand people milling around the square. We found a car parking space (wow!) and walked into a wall of noise: ear-splitting, recorded music and laughing, shouting voices. And many, many armed police. We found a quieter area with a gypsy singer and guitarist playing to a small but appreciative audience. He was a man in his sixties, his guitar almost as big as himself, and from his tiny frame came a voice of cracked sweetness, of night times singing round a campfire, of a thousand cigarettes.

We remembered the statues of rearing horses and huge bulls from our last visit but now, looking round, I understood the significance. They are about maleness and about domination, all too visible in the bars where young men, carefully coiffured, muscled bodies gleaming with body oil, drank beer, played guitars and paraded themselves loudly in front of the young women. Honestly, I only took a quick glance. The very air was laden with testosterone.

'Gazzie,' I said quietly, 'can we head home? I fear if I stay here a moment longer I shall grow testicles.'

With a horrified look downwards, he jumped in the car.

Tuesday. It's French conversation. Have I said before that I love this class? We sit in Bérènice's dining room, conversing in pretty awful French while her three cats put paws over their ears and hide under the chairs. We are a mixed bunch but we laugh till we ache. For my 'news for the week' I talked about our visit to Saintes-Maries-de-la-Mer. Fortunately testosterone and testicles are almost the same in French.

Wednesday found us back in Béziers for my ultrasound, so our friends wandered around while we experienced more of the French healthcare system. The scanner is in a modern building with free parking. We were seen early and whilst my doctor spoke no English and I, very little French, we seemed to manage. Though Gary said he did look surprised that I had all my clothes off when he was only looking at my stomach. Ten minutes later we left with my x-rays, his observations on what he had found, and lighter by seventy-five euros. Fair dos. We can reclaim three quarters of that. Gary translated the doctor's observations, then looked up the medical terms on Google, put on his doctor's uniform and told me what he'd found. Basically water retention, we think! We go to our doctor next week. Another twenty-five euros.

And so, dear readers, we arrive at the last day of our friends' visit. We had planned what we hoped would be a lovely surprise for them – a lunch cruise on the Canal du Midi. It was calm, relaxing and the weather was kind enough. Organisers Andrea and Jerry gave us a lovely cold buffet lunch and a choice of drinks. A perfect way to spend two and a half hours, with a commentary about the canal from Andrea, in English.

25

Jeux sans frontières

June 2018

The metallic tipped waves still move back and forth over the sand, though the children no longer scream with excitement. They play quietly beside their parents, all silhouetted against the sky. Soul music from the restaurants is playing unobtrusively, and Gazzie gets his long-held wish to stay on the beach until late.

We are in Spain. It seems highly unlikely to us native islanders that we drove for less than two hours and are in another country. No passports, no queuing, no delays. Just an EU sign. España. Though, subtly, the houses look different. The road signs too.

Just yards from the border is La Jonquera, a huge shopping area where everything is cheaper than in France. We drive past, looking forward instead to some Spanish culture, history, vistas. Until my eye is caught by a priapic sign to my left: Sex Toy

Supermarket. Come this way. *Naturellement, mes amis*[1], being now largely French, we made a '*pffffffffff,*' an extra long one for such a sin against good taste, and drove on by. One of us looked slightly put out.

The atmosphere, look and feel of the place started to change from the rounded hills and vineyards of Languedoc and the duck and *foie gras*[2], to forest, granite, *pa amb oli*[3], and hearty *paella* on the other side of the Pyrenees.

The Spanish do try to maintain their cultural traditions. Most hotels put on at least one flamenco night a week, an event greeted with respect by most tourists. Even though some bleary-eyed, beer-bellied Brit is sure to call out encouragingly, 'Show us your castanets, dahling,' whilst spilling San Miguel down his England football shirt.

We are staying in Roses, a delightful seaside town. I'm sure at the height of the season it is heaving, but on a weekend in early June it is just pleasantly full. Of course we go on the little tourist train. Red this time, and a disappointing song compared to the oompah one of the white train in Perpignan. '*Roseees Expreeess*' is played at every break in the commentary, and didn't quite cut it for us.

We walked because the great taxi conspiracy has moved to Spain. It is impossible to hire one. Anyone contemplating moving to Europe should open a taxi firm that operates at night. You'll make a fortune. While there, we walked four times from our hotel into town. Twenty-five minutes each way. I'm considering doing a marathon next year. I digress. We walked into town for our special meal. Pretty awful food. Shame really. But a very pretty restaurant.

The following day, we rose earlyish to do some sightseeing

---

1 Of course, my friends
2 Duck or goose liver
3 Majorcan or Catalan speciality of bread with oil

and there are many sights to be seen: the delightful towns of Collioure, Cadaqués, Figueras. We decided to visit Salvador Dalí's house in Portlligat. What the chauffeur didn't tell me, dear readers, was that this visit involved yet another hair-raising mountain range, with the now familiar cries of:

'Take me back down this instant.'

'No, the view is not beautiful. And anyway, I have my eyes closed.'

We looked at the house, but didn't go in because there was a long wait. And we were fascinated by the reminders of the recent Catalan independence bid. Very obviously it had massive support here because the mountains were covered in pro-independence slogans. Yellow ribbons adorned houses and boats. Most spectacularly, an ancient, enormous olive tree had ribbons on every single branch.

The stress of the high ride had rendered me a little tired, so following the inevitable tapas lunch, we went to a lovely beach and slept and read for five hours. Which is where we came in at the beginning of this chapter.

The rest of our little break will probably follow shortly, while I can still remember.

26

Secret Santa

June 2018

At a loose end on our last evening in Roses, we tried the in-house entertainment, a disco with a DJ so bad that neither the silent guests nor stoic staff could disguise their disbelief. But that old wartime spirit was still there, lurking in all of us, and soon everyone was jigging and twisting to whatever music he chose and I bet he went home on Cloud Nine. I hope so, because we all did.

We took the country route back after our day on the beach, via Figueras so that we could see the Dalí museum. There was nowhere to park because there was a big fête in the town gardens, so it was a quick photo of the outside of the museum with its rows of eggs round the top, and on to find a hostelry with eggs to consume. Sated, we travelled onwards through the elegant and sophisticated towns of Cadaqués and Collioure. I had done enough walking in Roses, so made notes and promises to return on foot. One day.

The border brought Hell Land – gaudy shops in La Jonquera packed with cars, and people buying cheap booze and cigarettes. A nightmare of consumerism. The border town of Le Perthus was no better – narrow roads, blocked by cars and vans, thousands of people with bulging shopping bags, litter and desperation. It would have been good to speed away, but the traffic was at a standstill. Finally we were through the gates of Hell and into the beautiful countryside of southern France. We drove along the coast road and the outside edge of the Étang Leucate de Salses, and began to ask ourselves why. We drove for maybe twenty miles through desertedness. Mile after mile (to be fair, kilometres) of houses, apartments. Empty. Even waterparks. Empty. Was this a case of poisoned water? Of involuntary euthanasia?

But wait. What did we see? A lone figure. As we grew closer (I promise you, my very dear readers, this is truth of the highest truthfulness) a man, dressed in red, carrying a black bag, was approaching a waste bin. Looking up, we saw he had long white hair and a long white beard. True as I am writing this. So, tell it not to children, but Father Christmas does not live in Lapland but in southern France. And who can blame him?

Also true, as above, the highest truthfulness and so on, further along the road we saw a younger man, coming from nowhere, going nowhere, dressed in red, black beard and hair. Son of . . . ?

We were now in danger of munching on car seats as it had been six hours since soggy toast and hardly coffee were consumed. Over the sand and sea holly we saw a sign. We called to Son of . . .

'Your secret is safe with us, *mais, le café, est il ouvert*? Is the café open?'

He said, '*Oui*'. Or was it, '*Ho, ho, oui*'?

We ran towards the entrance. *Nada. Rien.* Nothing. Just some surf boards and a sign saying *Pas CB*. No bank cards. So even if they had been open, we couldn't have partaken. Bloody Son of Father Christmas has a lot to learn.

Your weary travellers journeyed on, nor did our weariness prevent us from appreciating the scenery, but we had a hot date with a sizzling sausage in Laurens at 6.30 pm and now, as we drove into Leucate at 3.00 pm, hunger gnawed at our vitals, like the vulture gnaws on bone. We saw a sophisticated but empty restaurant. Open. It would do. We found a parking place in the next country and dragged ourselves towards the hunger haven. Then, suddenly, like a mirage in a desert, we saw a beach restaurant. Brain-numbing music poured out over the road. Were we disgusted? No! We were the disco divas of Roses. We swung by. We grabbed a table. Everyone around us, waiters and customers, were from another, much younger generation and yet they welcomed us like royalty. We feasted on oysters and something else revolting in a shell (Gaz) and chicken dippers (me). We watched the mating rituals of the young and smiled. And laughed. And thanked God for being alive. In front of us, a beautiful young woman sat crossed-legged, quietly watching and, I suppose, just being. She wore a white t-shirt with the slogan 'Amour is French.' Yup, that sums it up nicely.

We journeyed homewards to meet friends and enjoy, once again, the hospitality of Isla and Paul at Sarabande, with their gorgeous sausages and salads and wine. And dear old Gazzie, having been driving for three days, disengaged himself from the steering wheel. And so to bed.

27

Beyond the fringe

June 2018

My fringe hates this weather. I leave the house sleek and coiffed and within seconds my fringe has frizzed and there's a bleached Brillo Pad on my forehead. Any advice as to how to deal with this would be appreciated.

Yes, summer is well and truly here. Temperatures have been hovering around the 30s all week. With the heat came fringe problems, flies, mosquitoes, midges, bites, insomnia, body dysmorphia. And all possible compensatory factors in one bundle: granddaughter, Bethany, and lovely boyfriend.

In the weeks before they came, Gaz and I went into many a

huddle, worrying about where to take our athletic thrill-seekers. Suggestions included: mountain climbing, mountain biking, mountain skiing, in fact any mountain-related exercise; kayaking, canoeing, paddle boarding, water skiing, in fact any water-related exercise. Or chilling in Ibiza lounges and nightclubs, foam parties and discotheques. Though quite a lot of that stuff evidently happens hereabouts, we didn't know how to start finding it and, much as we love the kids, we didn't have a great desire to do so. The nearest we get to chill are the *guinguettes* or *pailottes* which are pop-up beach restaurants, built afresh every year in May and June with water, electricity, kitchens and toilets only to be completely dismantled in September. So, wearing our hippest beach wear, burka for me, knee-length shorts and panama hat and flips for Gaz (somewhere over the last twenty seasons his flops went missing) off we go to Mango Beach at Agde, with its South American vibe (such a useful word, 'vibe'). The youngsters paddled, said the water was freezing, sunbathed and chatted, while the Aged GrandPs lay like sperm whales on ultra-comfortable sunbeds. There is great food at reasonable prices and killer cocktails. Good French Immersion and a relaxing time away from their London jobs.

One thing not even considered on our List Of Things To Do With Grandchildren was wine tasting in a wine *domaine*. The great quaffing gene has affected every generation on my side of the family. Why did I imagine it would miss Beth? It would be a new experience for them both. The great Wine God, Mr. Bacchus, helpfully guided Mistress R. Soul right into the arms, or rather barrels, of the most charming and helpful *vigneron* in the world at Caveau Morin-Langaran, near Marseillan. Delicious wines too. We and the young quaffers shared a mixed box of six.

However, the general consensus was that the best day of all was at home, christening the dip pool, having a barbie, and singing along to Neil Diamond.

Another day of goodbyes loomed, but first to Marseillan for an amazing Pottery Fair, a fine lunch, and then to our second home, Béziers airport. We needn't have worried about what to do with the kids. It was great just being together again.

To ease the pain of parting from our lovely ones, we needed a treat. I had a scan booked for the next day in Béziers so we scoured the map southwards, found Argelès and booked a night in a hotel.

The scan took forever, but then we were off, heading for the Spanish border. It was getting late so we used the dreaded but fast motorway. The outside of the Hotel Mimosa (two stars) did not look promising, but once inside we found a very modern, very clean hotel with charming owners. A five minute wander took us to the sea. On our left was a deep and long sandy beach with a few beach bars, fringed with pine trees. To our right, oh my goodness, children's dream, our nightmare, dozens of twenty foot high plastic animals, fun fairs, loud music. We were not deterred! We were here for a change of scenery and we got it. After wandering around the garish shops stacked four deep back from the beach, we found a restaurant and ate well enough. The petulant screams of children and the yelping of hundreds of miniature dogs did not disturb our contentment as the sun went down over the beach.

We rose to a lovely al fresco breakfast and set off to explore the old town. It was market day. It was rammed. No matter, it was buzzy and interesting. We took our fill, then began the two hour journey back to Roujan, passing through Barcarès and Leucate which, as I told you, dear readers, were totally deserted only two weeks ago. Block upon block of empty apartments, whole camping villages unoccupied apart from the odd cat and Père Noël[1] and his family. Now the place was alive with frantic summer activity. Santa had, perhaps, escaped to Lapland, but

1 Father Christmas

the rest of the world had arrived! Was the Baobab Beach Bar open? It was. And we enjoyed a refreshing break there. Despite the waiter asking if he could borrow my fringe to clean his pans.

Hand-painted on some driftwood at the entrance to this bar is a sign: *Elle est pas belle, la vie?* Life's not bad is it? I'm inclined to agree. We are the lucky ones.

28

Falling to pieces

July 2018

The month of June left, quietly and elegantly, after the departure of a friend and neighbour from the UK. We had donned our Tour Guide uniforms and happily returned to some old haunts, including a more in-depth visit to Béziers.

Somehow I have neglected Béziers in my little travelogues and yet we go there often with our visitors. One of the oldest cities in France, dating from 575 BC, it is a city whose ancient buildings and monuments are so beautifully preserved you can literally touch the past as you wander round. Grubby suburban streets give way to the Allée Paul Riquet dominated by the stunning Municipal Theatre, tree-lined central promenade and elegant shops. The Allée leads on to the recently completed plaza with its musical fountains. Even I thought it worth struggling up the cobbles to the grounds of the glorious Cathédrale Saint Nazaire et Saint Celse de Béziers to see the vista over the city. But imagine my chagrin, dear readers, when I boarded the little tourist train and discovered I could have avoided the burn of my thighs and the scream of my corns caused by walking the cobbly, steep streets and seen it all in the relative comfort of the little electric cattle truck which transports you to places which you might otherwise have missed, like the beautiful Poets Park. Being a Tuesday, and therefore b*rocante* market day, we later strolled among the antique stalls and spent a happy, dusty hour fingering the past and looking aghast at the prices.

After a soul-brimming drive to Rivesaltes, near Perpignan, and a taste of the dessert wine for which it is famous, we deposited our friend (she was willing) and returned home to prepare for the next adventure.

Three old (as in long-term and, well, lots of years) friends were next on the visitors list. Aged between eighty and ninety but sparky, bright and intelligent, the women – Sheila, Esther and Annie, very affectionately known as She 'n Es 'n Annie – do have some mobility issues which ruled out staying with us at our rented house. A local couple offered us their zany, attractive house with a swimming pool at a good price. We checked out ease of access and the safety of the very few stairs and deemed the place suitable. Then came the news that She had fallen in her garden in Suffolk and broken her wrist. Despite this, the brave explorers were determined to have their holiday in France.

Truth to tell, we were a bit concerned, but our worries vanished when the three arrived and were visibly excited with their holiday home. We shared a meal, reminiscing over holidays past, and were making our way to bed when She slipped and fell. Again. A night of pain for her and concern for the rest of us until at

6.00 am we called an ambulance. Gazzie and Es followed it and returned with the news that She had not only a broken left wrist but a broken right arm too. One of my asides: I wouldn't have minded following that ambulance because the paramedics were gorgeous! What a brave woman She is. No moans, no fuss. In two days she had been operated on. In three days, released from hospital. Annie, meanwhile, was suffering from back pain and the heat which hovered in the upper 30s and spent long periods laid out in bed. Es had also slipped but carried on with a badly bruised coccyx. Given this worrying pattern of falls, Gaz forced me to don body armour and slide around the house and garden on my bottom. We forswore alcohol.

Out came Gazzie's doctor's uniform, on went his face mask, and he spent happy hours dabbing here, bandaging there, testing for rising temperatures both on the patients and on meteorological sites. He strode around the villa as if the sole House Doctor on duty on a Saturday night in A&E. His patients, when they could express themselves, treated him as if he were Mother Teresa risen from the dead to tend them.

Obviously our itinerary was vastly curtailed and several outings cancelled, but in between visits to hospital, we did manage to take Annie and Es on that little train around Béziers. Try as we might, though, our *joie de vivre* was diminished by concern for, and the absence of, Sheila.

The day before departure, She expressed a wish to see the sea, so with the other two still *hors de combat*[1], we took a gentle ride to Marseillan and ate mussels on the quayside. We touched on our dreams, we whispered 'if onlys'. There was hesitant planning, firmer intentions, nodding to the past, welcoming the future. Talks of friends here and friends gone. Of families and the familiar. We condensed our drifting holiday talk into these very few hours.

---

1 out of action

We dropped *Les Girls* off at the airport and watched in amazement as She was winched up into the plane and Annie, despite her bad back, zig-zagged across the tarmac pushing Es in a wheelchair. So even their departure was fraught with danger. And farce.

We hope that, with time, this holiday will be the one that provokes the most laughter, albeit in retrospect. What better tribute could there be?

And in preparation for that time, the grapes grow on the vine, plumptious with promise.

29

Allez les bleus

July 2018

The plane that took away 'the girls' brought in our daughter, Sara. She just can't keep away. What balm for the soul. Her cheerful, dear little face did much to assuage the worries of the previous week.

No sooner were her bags dumped indoors than we were off again because Sara wanted to watch the World Cup football match between France and Belgium in a bar in France. We checked into our local bar.

'*Non*,' said the patron. 'I am closing.'

We did a French '*pffff*' with raised shoulders, found somewhere to eat, and caught up with the match on our phones.

Sara has visited so often now, I am very glad to say, that she tells us where she wants to go and Gaz has added her to his car insurance so she can relieve him of some of the driving. But we did have some new experiences for her. First up – Pézenas has begun its Friday Estivales which run throughout the summer. There are food stalls, live music and a great atmosphere, all supported by local people. The main street is lined with *vignerons* with their stalls, offering wine tastings. You buy a glass for €5 and get two free tastings. After that, taste as many as is sensible at €2 a refill. Honestly, the lengths we go to in supporting the local economy. It would be rude to try just one, too rude; one has to give one's custom to as many as possible. Ignoring any stall selling frog legs or oysters, we joined the longest queue for chips. Worth the fifteen minute wait though.

Sara was here for Bastille Day which every village celebrates. Our landlady had whetted our appetite with tales of food and wine (of course it rains wine in these parts), live music and fireworks. With giggly tummies, we wandered downtown at eight-ish, worrying that we wouldn't get a seat. We listened out for jolly voices to direct us to Funsville. Despite the lack of any such voices we found the venue. Two bouncy castles, a stand serving hummus, an empty sound stage and the ever-present wine stands. Twenty large tables, two security guards. And twelve people.

'Well, that wasn't very well-supported,' we mumbled into our beards as we wandered back home. On the way, we passed a packed restaurant. No, honestly, we do not spend our lives in restaurants. Just when people visit us.

'Daft not to go in,' we said.

We got the last table, had one course and a *pichet* of wine. And then . . . those jolly voices we had listened for earlier echoed past the restaurant and excited children carrying lanterns thronged the street. Quick! We paid the bill and followed the miniature Pied Pipers back to Funsville. There was great music. There were amazing fireworks. The whole village was there. *Vive*

La France[1]! Another little foible in the foibleiest country in Christendom is that even child-centred events start at silly o'clock and if food is involved you'll be eating chair legs before anything sustaining is served.

Because we had enjoyed a lovely day at a *paillote* with the grandchildren, we headed for a different one with Sara. New to us was La Voile Rouge, near Sète. Lovely food, cool music and comfy beds. We arrived early, played in the silky warm sea and enjoyed a light lunch. Then a movement of bodies and a raising of voices alerted us to a TV and the broadcasting of the World Cup final between France and Croatia. We joined in, cheering with the French when their team scored, and being part of their celebratory hugs and shouts when they won. I really like the huggy thing (I'm using the upward interrogative of young-person-speak).

We drove home with the evening sun slipping towards the horizon, the car windows open and our journey accompanied by the peep of car horns and the shouts of the people. They waved flags, arms, legs . . . anything waveable. Almost. We joined the victory parade down Pézenas main street where the joy was contagious. *Vive la France! Vive le Royaume-Uni! Vive le monde!*[2]

And, yes, I know what I said about restaurants, but you may like to know this for when you visit, dear friends. I had heard of a restaurant in the hills in a village called Vailhan. Built into a seventeenth century presbytery above a reservoir, Äponem is owned and cheffed by Amélie Darvas and Gaby Benicio, ex-Paris restaurateurs. I booked.

I knew nothing about it, except that the previous chef was good, not cheap but good value. It was our goodbye-to-daughter meal. We asked for the menu. There was a lot of French talky

---

1 Long live France
2 Long live France! Long live the UK! Long live the world!

but no recognisable food choices. Just €55 for six somethings and €75 for ten somethings. We needed a drink. Picked up the wine list, desperately looking for a *pichet* of house white. *Rien.* Nothing. Cheapest wine was €30. We looked at each other, white-faced and wriggling in our seats.

'Well, I don't mind walking out and saying it was a terrible mistake,' I said.

'OK, let's,' we agreed.

Then Sara. 'Well, I didn't buy that dress I liked.' True. Though she did later. 'And that meal on the beach cost almost as much.'

'And we didn't spend much last week when the girls were here,' we added.

All totally spurious fiscal arguments, with no basis in sound economics. But we began to feel better and better.

'Well, if we have the cheaper, six-course option and the cheapest bottle of wine, we'll actually be saving money.'

'Yeah, why not? We deserve it.'

Meanwhile, the attentive waitress, Gaby, was still waiting. We deliberated so long that she had fallen asleep and was softly snoring.

'We're going for it,' we said.

Obviously impressed by our cheffy terminology, Gaby awoke with a start and returned to efficient waitress mode. 'Each course,' she informed us, 'is part of a journey, a story,' and we should, 'relax and enjoy the experience.'

Hoping that my, 'What a load of codswallop,' thinking was not visible on my face, we smiled and gave her our, 'Get the bloody €30 bottle of wine on the table,' look. And then, dear readers, it became apparent that we were total philistines. Yes, of course, we know that what we paid for the meal could feed a family of four for a week. And yes, we do feel privileged. And yes, we will be paying for it for the next six months. But none of us, in our lives, had experienced the food sensations that we experienced that night, served such that each plate was a work of art. Wine was almost immaterial (thank goodness) but the whole experience was truly exceptional. Heston Blumenthal eat your heart out. Well, I wouldn't put it past him.

At last, in the cradle of gastronomy, an incomparable taste experience.

30

Some like it hot

August 2018

We slither into shadows like ne'er-do-wells avoiding the police. Our heads are covered. Sweat pours from our faces like colourless blood from an invisible wound. We seek watering holes like weary buffalo. Those we pass speak the same words in parched whispers through cracked lips. 'Turn. Off. The. Sun.'

We pay fortunes to stay a while in air-conditioned shops, cinemas, houses. We form undying friendships with anyone who has a pool. We sit in sealed, dark houses in front of fans whizzing out air only one degree lower than the ambient temperature. There is no energy to swat away flies or mosquitos. Summer 2018 in Languedoc. And most of Europe. Three weeks to date with temperatures in the high 30s and rising.

We head for the coast to find some respite. A first-time visit to Rochelongue, a tourist venue but none the worse for that. Miles and miles of sandy beaches, hundreds and hundreds of people, and yet the beach does not feel crowded or loud. Beach Club L'Infinit has the best lunch menu so far, apart from the sole running out just as I was about to order. (Isn't it hell, darlings, when that happens?) The busy chef surprises us by shelling my prawns and all the staff are delightful. As is the lovely sea breeze.

The following day, still seeking solace from the searing sun (I love a bit of sibilance) we head for the hills. Oh, my goodness me. I had been experiencing another little bout of homesickness but the journey towards Lac Salagou lifts my spirits. The vineyards peter out, giving way to wheat fields, blue mountains and pink and yellow rock terrain.

And every so often, like *amuses bouches* for the eyes (*amuses yeux?*), little villages appear, exciting because we feel we've discovered them. Pézènes-les-Mines is awe-inspiring, a medieval village dominated by its eleventh/twelfth century chateau. For over a thousand years the villagers have been producing Faugères wine from their vineyards. Their ancient buildings tumble over one another and down into the wooded valley below.

Reluctantly we leave, and continue to Lac Salagou, eyes wide with wonder, brows unusually perspiration-free with the air con on full blast. You would think we might suffer beauty overload, but each new vista and village finds a place in our hearts. Whilst Lac Salagou is man-made, Man has done his very best to make a thing of beauty. The lake, created in 1968, regulates the River Salagou which can flood in the autumn. We approach the lake from its quieter side and sit shaded from the sun in one of the lake's *guinguettes*, Relais Nautique. A few folk swim and paddle but nothing interrupts the peace. We continue, driving right round the lake, taking in the busier water sports area and more sophisticated restaurants, until we are overlooking the village of Celles.

Celles was evacuated when the area was flooded to create the lake, although the water did stop short of the village. However, apart from the occupied *Mairie* and the church, the houses are falling very slowly into disrepair. We have heard that the village is to be repopulated. It would be wonderful if the homes are offered to the families who were forcibly evacuated, but I suspect they will be gentrified into expensive holiday homes.

Gazzie chooses a hair-raising journey home on an unmade road right round the lake. We spot a sign for Saint-Guilhem-le-Désert.

'Shall we?' asks the driver.

'*Oui*,' says pretentious passenger.

We decide that the whole area, one of the most popular tourist destinations in Languedoc – the medieval village, the Clamouse Cave, the Gorges de l'Hérault, the Pont du Diable – is worth a visit but there is no room to park or walk or see, so we drive through and will return out of season. You will come with us, dear readers, if you so wish.

Despite never-ending flesh-roasting temperatures, we join the local villagers who celebrate the certainty of these warm evenings with weekly festivals, fêtes and fairs where we drink, eat and dance wildly. Well, I do. All those things I have described to you previously on these *brasucade* nights. Fires are lit on pavements (as if it's not hot enough) to cook game, chicken and fish. There is live music and the ever-present *vignerons* offer their wines for us to taste. So civilised. So not health and safety. But if we are to immerse ourselves in the culture of our neighbouring villages, it is incumbent upon us to attend.

31

Save me, save me, save me from this cheeze

August 2018

I came within a whisker of being done for shoplifting today.

Short version: Go to Aldi for cheap Prosecco. See Babybel cheeses. 'Ooh I used to love those, Gaz.'

'Get some,' he says. 'Only one euro sixty.' Generous to a fault, our Gaz.

I do. Open one in the car. 'Urghh. Why do I think I liked those?' Throw them in my shopping basket.

Go to SuperU as couldn't get our favourite coffee in Aldi. As usual, pick up other stuff. Go to self-checkout.

'Ha ha,' says so-called 'Here to 'effing Help, Smiley-Face Person'. 'Why is zeeze in zee basket?'

'Got them in Aldi,' I say with a British Colonial sneer.

'Receipt?' she says.

I now have three snotty women and a man with a walkie-talkie around me. And is that a gun, or is he just pleased to nab me?

'In the car?' I say, hopefully, in French, as if to prove how innocent and law-abiding I am.

'Fetch!' says Walkie-Talkie Man while relaying this to Paris Police HQ. I wagged my tail and sped off to fetch.

I return from car. 'Can't find it,' I say.

'You pay then,' says Walkie-Talkie man.

'Whateva. It's only one euro bloody sixty,' I mutter.

Officious woman comes and grabs my Babybels. Tries to scan them. The little darlings will not scan. She gets on phone. To Interpol. Another officious Mother of Satan comes over, grabs my Babybels and goes off. Returns. There are now FIFTY French people glaring at the thieving foreigners.

'OK,' She says. 'You keep Babybels and go.'

Obviously they wouldn't scan because they don't sell the bloody things. With a small show of temper I throw the offending balls into the shopping basket. This sets off a screeching alarm because an unscanned item has entered the basket. Or Swag Bag as we now call it. I bought that bag to save the children of Mozambique. See where that act of charity has got me.

No apology. No smile. No helping hand. Nada. 'SuperU: U ain't so bloomin' Super now.' Carrefour for me from now on.

I am a marked woman.
APPROACH WITH CAUTION
Baby 'Bad-Ass' Bel.
Inside for crimes against real cheese.

32

But oh oh those su-ummer ni-ights

August 2018

However hard we try with our French Language CDs and in our conversation classes, we still panic when locals speak to us. We have had several halting conversations with our lovely neighbour, who makes valiant attempts to use the odd word of English to help me out. Not so her husband, however – evidently a man of few words even in his native tongue. But as the old adage goes, 'actions speak louder than words', and they regularly call round with vegetables from their allotment and fresh trout caught on their fishing trips. I have tried to express how welcome this makes us immigrants feel.

Segueing nicely into other welcoming people, we must stand

up for the people of Puissalicon. A group of us Brits attended their *Nuit des Vins*[1]. I know, wine again, but that is the *raison d'être*[2] of this area. The anticipation is palpable as the harvest begins. At all festivals, wines from the local *domaines* are sold, and the events nicely dressed up with tapas and wonderful music and dancing. Everyone gets up to do the Line Dances and smiles replace words in a warm atmosphere of goodwill. The French in this area seem to love Line Dancing and everyone from two to ninety join in. And what a rich harvest for those watching. On the non-health-and-safety bonfires were cooked quail, sausages, pork, mussels and *frites*[3] which were served with salads and cheese. And, between ourselves, wine at €2 a glass. And the *pièce de résistance*[4], as we say in this country, was the appearance of the village mascot. Most villages have one. Roujan has the hedgehog, a huge representation carried high at festivals. I confess I am not sure what the huge blue animal of Puissalicon was, but it was welcomed with the passion and fervour normally reserved for pop stars.

I promise we will never tire of visiting all the *fêtes* or festivals. I know, dear readers, you think it's because of the wine, but truthfully it is because the enthusiasm and hard work of the organisers and the total support of the villagers illustrates, for me, the essential goodness of most of humankind. And I like the unsophisticated way they're put together with the *fêtes* taking place on *boules* courts, car parks, in town squares. There are old, rickety tables and chairs, and no charge to attend. Every age group is represented and children play and dance around the adults until late in the evening.

I pondered on such matters whilst listening to live lunchtime

---

1 Night of wine
2 Reason for existing
3 Chips
4 The most memorable part, the masterpiece

jazz in a small bar, as part of the St. Thibéry Jazz Festival. People here put so much effort and hard work into preparing and presenting their festival. They even produce a special wine for the duration, in this case, Cap Jazz. The jazz event was mellow with a very gifted double bass player, and we were all given a jazz hat. And more and more people were watched. Simple pleasures.

Sometimes, when Gazzie is playing golf, I meet up with friends. I have friends near Clermont-l'Herault who suggested we meet for lunch at Villeneuvette, somewhere I had never been. Villeneuvette is a small preserved village of buildings initially erected in the seventeenth-century to create a royal linen-making factory for Louis XIV, and was unusual in providing accommodation and amenities for its workers on site. It now has a hotel and restaurant and also around sixty-five permanent residents who form a very strong community. And very pretty it is too. And the quality of our lunch matched the beauty of the setting.

I have noted in the past, dear readers, some French idiosyncrasies, and in that past have *vived la différence*. Here are three more, observed only this week.

So. Number one. Last evening, we were at a dinner party with French, British (just us two) and Zimbabweans. One of the guests was Max, a two year old French boy. Max stood by Gary's chair looking at him with adoration. Gaz, unaware, suddenly pulled back his arm to illustrate something he was saying and smacked Max full in the face with his elbow. Now my acquaintance with (mostly British) children suggests they would have made the most of the attention of the wine-imbibing dinner guests and screamed loudly for as long as they had breath in their bodies. Not so this little boy. With the dignity of a very dignified person, Max climbed onto Mama's lap, put two fingers in his mouth and stared at his attacker with a look of benevolent puzzlement. Or possibly concussion. I haven't checked.

Here's another. I do miss the politeness taken to ludicrous levels in Britain. So, for instance, I know I'm carrying some extra weight but lovely Brits would, I hope, just say, 'You look well.' Here, I go into a dress shop and a stick insect sidles up to me, points imperiously at a rack of six bell tents in various dark colours and says, '*Les grandes tailles*' (big sizes). Yesterday took the biscuit (very fattening, biscuits). I picked out a nice red dress the size of a barrage balloon and was carrying it towards the changing rooms when a young sales person ran up to me. '*Non, non,*' says she. 'No good for you. You have the big boobies.' And as if to emphasise the point, in front of all the other customers, she poked my big boobies and took the dress away. I'd rather have the girls at Zara sniggering behind their hands as I try to squeeze into one of their tiny jackets.

And finally. I was told that the French, in general, hate speed cameras. As happens in many parts of France, a camera placed on one of the country roads nearby was knocked over, set fire to and left, only three days after it was installed. And two weeks later, there it lies.

So, dearest readers, ponder along with me if you will. Am I describing the national traits of a whole culture? Or did I chance on a few insensitive salespeople, one stoic little boy, and a person with speed camera phobia? Because aren't we all universally unique? I do hope so.

33

Ants in our pants

August 2018

Gazzie has decided to make Mistress R. Soul not only legal, but French. How she will react remains to be seen.

'If you live here for more than six months you're supposed to get your car registered in France,' says Gaz. It has been eight months since our arrival.

You may remember, dear readers, that my fiscal acumen is pretty shaky so we did a pro and con exercise. Most unlike us. Compared with the English system, registration is about £700 per year cheaper. No more road tax. MOTs are required every two years. Insurance is half the cost charged by our specialist insurer in England. If we add in the costs of returning to the UK by car once a year for MOT, service and tax, it is, as we now fiscally astute folks say, a No Brainer.

We started by asking advice from expats and from searching expat online forums. Most reported it was easy. Ten minutes with the friendly folk at the local *Mairie*, pay your money and send off the forms. Robert *est votre oncle*[1].

Dear readers, have you already guessed that it wouldn't be

---

1 Bob's your uncle

like that for us? The French have just discovered the power of the computer so you have to register cars through the national agency, ANTS. And of course France has a totally deserved reputation for excessive bureaucracy – copies or originals of everything, in triplicate, are demanded for the simplest thing. So being online means going paperless. Right? You know the answer.

Despite which, Gazzie went to the *Mairie* for the simple, first step of obtaining a mysterious document called the *Quitus Fiscale* (QF). He was told he needed to go to the Béziers Centre of Finances. The QF is a document that proves you've bought the car and paid the VAT. We have proof in the form of a purchase invoice and receipt but they want this in translation. When asked why they wanted NUMBERS translated, Gallic shoulders were shrugged together with the response to all questions whose answer is not actually known. *'Parce que'* . . . Because.

So for an outlay of forty quid we learnt that the French for VAT is *'TVA'* and the French word for invoice is *'facture d'achat'*.

At the Centre of Finances desk, the non-English-speaking and very pleasant lady gave us a list of required documents, a list obviously newly provided by the modernised ANTS. In his best pigeon French, Gary showed her the smaller requirement list taken from the government website and asked why we needed the seven piece list when the government website said four. Her marvellously French explanation was, 'I don't know why but I'm sure there must be a reason.' At least she didn't say, *'Parce que,'* but she did phone someone else. He said he would come down.

A middle-aged, friendly man, definitely old school, whisked us into a private room, asked questions, and when he understood the car was ten years old and we were not international luxury car smugglers and tax evaders, he gave the ubiquitous *'pffff'* sound that only the French can make when faced with life's ridiculousness. He took only four documents and said we'd get the QF within a few days. Success!!

Errr. You might think so but then ANTS got their hooks into this old-fashioned process. We got a phone call saying that we couldn't make the arrangements at Béziers because it had to be at our nearest tax office which was Pézenas. Off we dutifully went to Pez and asked for a *rendezvous*[2] (RDV) to get the QF. They gave us that list again. 'You have to do it online,' they said. (Bloody ANTS again!) And so the farce really began.

Gaz emailed Pez to ask for a RDV for a QF. Attached seven documents (!).

Response: You need to make a tax declaration.

Gaz: Only just decided to live here, only been here for a few months which is too short a time to declare tax. The attached documents prove I bought the car in England and tax has been paid so can I have a QF? All patiently emailed with only a bit of swearing.

Response: You've got to declare tax. Can't have a QF without a tax declaration.

Gaz: Government website says four documents. You say seven. Don't understand why I need to be a tax resident.

Response: Here's the list of the seven documents needed.

Gaz: I can't do a tax return because I'm not a tax resident. New French phrase acquired: *semblent tourner en rond*. Going round in circles.

The French cavalry was called upon to deal with the stupid English.

Capitaine's response: My colleague has given you the list. No documents equals no QF. No tax declaration equals no QF.

These emails took place over three days but Gaz thought he had found a fatal flaw and could slay the mighty dragon of French bureaucracy with his cleverness.

---

2 Appointment

Gaz: But I need to have been here a year to do a tax return and I've only been here for six months. The law says I must register my car after six months but I can't register it without QF so you are making my car illegal.

Response: Regularise your tax affairs and you can have a QF.

Gaz: Is there someone there who can help me regularise my tax affairs, preferably who speaks English. Or I can bring someone who speaks French. Can I have an RDV?

Response: Ring this number. (THAT list was attached again!!) Two months later.

Gaz: I've declared my taxes but I don't know what to do now? Can I have a QF?

Response: We haven't kept the documents you attached to your email. Can you send them with a copy of your tax declaration?

Gaz: I delivered it by hand to your office. I didn't keep a copy. But I have received two phone calls asking for some details about the declaration so I know someone there has it. Do I have to wait for my tax notice or can I get a tax number now and get my QF?

Response: Send us the receipt/proof of your tax return. (Attached was ANOTHER list of documents needed!!!!)

Gaz: Here's a list of what I delivered. No receipt was given.

Response: I think you'd better have an RDV.

Went to RDV, had to copy three bits of information from documents we had already sent them, in Gaz's own writing, onto a carbon copy pad which our kind bureaucrat tore out and gave to me. Took ten minutes . . .

. . . and four months.

The Mistress fought bravely against the operation to remove her British number plates, making it worse for herself as the whole nasty business took hours. And both she and I felt a bit like traitors as the men put the French ones in place. After a few days, however, she was full of herself, French *chanteuses*[3] played on her radio and her exhaust fumes had the distinct aroma of Gauloises.

---

3 Singers

34

Bullocks

August 2018

There is a respite from the brain-frying heat.

We set off for Vendres Plage where already there is a *fin de siècle*[1] feel about the beaches – fewer children, fewer people altogether. On Saturday we go to the last *brasucade* in Puissalicon, and on Sunday the last Sizzling Sausage evening at the Sarabande vineyard. Soon will come the seasonal collecting of the grapes and the pressing of the olives to which you, dear readers, will be invited through these pages.

And as August sizzles out, we are stocking up with logs and making sure the house is as lovely as when we arrived in December, because our days in this rented place are numbered.

---

1 Turn of the century

And we have been making decisions. Our intention was to stay in France for a year. Gazzie has taken to the French life like a *canard* to *l'eau*[2], wholeheartedly embracing it. I have had more of a struggle and yet, in some ways I am more integrated than he is with my creative writing classes and my book group. But I still change my mind more often than I change my knickers. I do pro and anti lists. To be honest, and far be it from me to disrespect my homeland, my life here is richer. Living in another country and in warmer weather makes me more outgoing. The upshot of our discussions is that I have agreed to stay for another year. Which means we have to find another tenant for our house in England and somewhere else to live in France.

With amazing speed we do both.

In November we must move away from this little jewel of a house with its beautiful views across the countryside to an ancient, though modernised house in the centre of the village of Gabian. We can walk to the baker and a little grocery shop and, lord help us, a bar and restaurant. This medieval village lies in a valley defined by the River Thongue with its Roman bridge and allotment-filled banks. There we will be looking at old tiles and stone instead of the changing panoply of the Roujan countryside. So, a very different living space but I hope we'll be as content there as we have been in Debbi's house. We shall miss our lovely neighbours, Babeth and Paul, their generous gifts, and our very hesitant conversations. Today they brought us a tray of fresh green and purple figs. For a farewell gift, we bought them a Make Your Own Dog Kit. The finished dog is, thank heavens, without a barking mechanism.

And, since we are staying, we must continue our immersion in French culture. Do you know that bullfighting is still legal in France and practised in some towns in the south like Nîmes and Arles in Provence? Neither of us had ever attended a bull-related

2 Duck to water

event so we decided to go to the Bull Run in Tourbes. There was some trepidation on my part. Although not the world's most passionate animal lover, I do abhor all forms of cruelty.

So here we are. And although the horses and the four young bullocks might prefer to be chomping away merrily in a field somewhere, they appear in fine fettle as they gallop two hundred yards up the main road and back again. Not so much a nod to bullfighting as an acknowledgement of the lives of the *gardians* who tend the black bulls and white horses of the Camargue wetlands. (Remember our visit there earlier in the year, readers? I do hope you are cross-referencing). It is interesting rather than exciting and I fantasise about a handsome *gitan* scooping me up onto his white horse, taking me to his caravan and playing his guitar for me around the campfire. Spookily, after the thunder of hooves dies down, real gypsy guitarists serenade the crowds as we make our way to the food and wine tents. Honestly, you can't even go to the tip without a food and wine tent popping up. No coincidence that Michelin Tyre Man was French. I could be mistaken for him after eight months in France.

In most villages, at every festival, it is traditional for some of the men to dress as women. I have no idea why. Perhaps they just like it. In Roujan, the men have a very sophisticated outfit of white skirts, blue tops, white socks and shoes. Here, the Minettes of Tourbes sport luminous green wigs, grass skirts, bra tops, silver handbags and shoes. What is it with me? I found them strangely attractive, in a green sort of way. I took lots of photos which I studied minutely in the privacy of my room. I don't think I deserved the terse reply to my request to join the troupe. 'You're not from Tourbes,' they said, 'and you lack at least one essential of an all-male ensemble.'

35

These golden days
I'll spend with you

September 2018

That beautiful old classic, *September Song*, is playing in the background, reminding me that 'the days grow short when we reach September'. And so they do and the people of Languedoc start to prepare for winter. Yet the old folk still sit outside their houses or in the town squares, gossiping and enjoying the slanting light and kinder sun.

We take up the rhythm of the seasons with our neighbours and feel pleasure in being outside, the air so much fresher now and the white-hot heat of August paled to gold. People open their windows and door shutters during the day. In England, when it's hot, we throw open our doors and windows.

In France they do the opposite – shut them and close fast the shutters, giving the houses a sightless look. Our neighbourhood has a friendlier feel with the houses' eyes wide open. Even now it would be wonderful to have a cool pool in which to dip a toe or two, but despite a parade of Fixers coming to its aid, the water in our dip pool is still luminous green and has the consistency of porridge. It is a happy breeding ground for a whole variety of wildlife of the bitey/stingy kind. I have a feeling we won't be dipping anything in it while we are here.

Like withholding water from a dying man, the doctor forbids Gazzie from any more sunbathing. You can hear his cries, can't you? But a vicious heat rash has given him the appearance of a pinkly-scaled reptile and whilst I still love him, the local children and animals recoil in horror. We hide in the shady, air-conned coolness of the car. But then it seemed foolish just to sit there, so we whispered the words Mistress R. Soul loves to hear. 'Off we go.'

We took a breathtaking ride across La Route Causses et Vallées de l'Hérault, a UNESCO World Heritage site. Walls of green forest parted to reveal limestone plateaux of poetic beauty.

'Ooooh look, Gaz,' I say. 'There's a circus over that way. Must be a permanent one as it's on this map.'

'Look it up on Google, Wife.'

It did feel odd having a conversation with a pink reptile but as you've now realised, dear readers, very little fazes me. Except, maybe . . . dogs, animals of any sort, walking, heat, grubby hotels and heights.

'Says here, Gaz, the Cirque de Navacelles is a series of limestone gorges. Plus lots of stuff about views from the top. So not a circus at all but something which involves walking, nay, probably climbing, and then looking down or up. I think me vertigo's coming on. Down, Gazzie. Down, boy.'

Sorry, dear readers, your tour guide failed you a bit there.

But, should you go, do take photos and send them to me. I'll look at those.

And on across the high plains, through villages of flowers and stone, stray cats rolling in dusty streets, horses and cattle flicking their tails . . . and not a single human being for mile upon mile upon mile until we reached our final destination of La Couvertoirade in the Aveyron department. This very well preserved, fortified town was owned by the Knights Templar in the twelfth and thirteenth centuries and then by the Knights of St. John of Jerusalem. It was pleasant indeed to wander through those ancient streets, now kept alive by craftspeople working with enamel, clay, fabric and more. I imagine in the height of the tourist season its narrow streets are impassable, and probably impossible, but on a quiet September day it was easy to imagine (for me, though not for Gaz) that I was the wench of some knight shortly to return from protecting Christian pilgrims somewhere, accompanied by a pinkly-scaled reptile who was her manservant. Happy daze.

I'm learning to sketch. I'm pretty hopeless but I enjoy it, and our teacher, Annette, winkles out any microcosm of talent that might be lurking. Mine is still very lurky. Our lovely Sara, back for the sixth time, came with me to the second lesson. I loved sitting in the sunshine, looking rather fetching in my beret and smock, but looking fetching doth not an artist make and my naive efforts did not satisfy me. Evidently everyone has something they excel at. I'm still searching for my something.

Multi-talented daughter suggested a return visit to Lake Salagou to check out the water sports on offer. (As I have said, swapped at birth, surely?) Seeking some respite from the sweaty, energetic people doing all sorts of stuff on the water, my eyes were drawn again to the pink hills surrounding the lake where thousands of messages are written with white stones, everything from 'Jim was 'ere' to lines of poetry. I love to touch these lines of other people's lives.

129

The seasons of the vine create the pattern of a year in Languedoc, and how quickly that pattern has become part of the lives of the newcomers who have settled here. It's 5.45 am. I've never seen that time on a clock before. Sara, Gary and I have risen in the dark because we have offered our grape-picking services to Isla and Paul, *vignerons* of the Sarabande vineyard where we enjoyed Sunday's sizzling sausages. It is already 22°C as we join a small caravan of vehicles heading to their vineyard. Dawn breaks over the hills, thankfully illuminating our path as we walk deep into the countryside, past wild boar spooked by the three springer spaniels who race alongside us. During my time here I have visited vineyards every month to photograph the progress of the vine, from the stark, black stunted branches of winter to the first tiny, lime green leaves to the nascent bunches of tiny grapes. Now, that ripe bounty is cradled in dark green leaves which protect it and keep it from falling. It feels like coming to the end of a story, a time when the hard work and vigilance of the *vigneron* is rewarded with a plump and plentiful harvest. And we rookie English, who have tended little more than a flower border, have come to help pick the grapes. It feels good. It feels relevant. We feel included. But no time for poetic reflection, we are here to work. We set to at a cracking pace after two seconds of training. The sun starts to climb high behind us. And boy, do we labour. And boy, do we love it. We reckon we pick enough for two hundred bottles (it might be twenty, I'm not good with noughts), before the break for coffee and cake. And, despite being a lady of uncertain years, my picking rate increases rapidly when I spot the beautiful, muscly, smiley young man who picks up the full crates and hoists them onto his fine shoulders. I have a photo somewhere. Oh, silly me, there it is, stuck to the computer. And so we help bring the wine harvest home. As we wearily retrace our path, despite aching backs and red wine stains we feel a visceral pleasure in being part of this centuries-old method of harvesting the grape (no machines used here) ready for the next stage of pressing to extract the juice. And, after all, we do have a vested interest in ensuring a plentiful supply of wine for the coming year. On the road, the kindly council, ever conscious of our safety, has erected road signs: *chaussée glissante vendanges.* Loosely translated, 'road slippery with wine.' I know that feeling!

Tomorrow is my birthday. We have been here for nine months. Very soon we start the search for another home:

a) because our landlady wants her home back

b) because we have decided to extend our stay for another year.

Gazzie fell in love with this place almost immediately. It's taking longer for me to be seduced. I've shared with you my homesickness, feelings which puzzle me because friends and family fly over frequently. My homesickness, however, is not only for people, but for a way of life which is still there, just over the Channel. And also a world away. I surprised myself when I finally agreed to stay. But then, dear readers, I have been surprising myself rather a lot lately.

36

Red red wine

October 2018

We came upon a scene reminiscent of *Murders on the Rue Morgue*.

We have called into Sarabande to check on the grapes we harvested. Isla and Paul welcome us with open arms that are stained deep crimson, as are their legs and every other unprotected part of their bodies. They tread their grapes in the traditional way or use a huge old wooden wine press. Content that our contribution has been treated with respect, we escape the carnage for the vineyards themselves.

And the vines are dying back, having given up their fruits for our enjoyment. There will be a short respite for Isla and Paul before their work begins once more in preparing for next year's crop, a ten month cycle so far from bare black branches in January to the first press. All by hand for this young couple, using traditional methods of wine production.

I had always believed in the old adage 'never go back', the

implication being that you will be disappointed. Because we want to share the lovely places we know, we do go back with our visitors and honestly discover new things every time. So, back to Béziers we go to show Maz and Johnny the newly completed palazzo with its musical fountains and water walkways. You can visit Béziers twenty times and still find new areas to admire. The reason for going on a Tuesday is to browse the antique stalls. In a reverse role situation, one of the very French stallholders insists on photographing Marilyn! We eat in the square below the cathedral – the best mussels I have ever eaten. *Gratinéed*[1] but plump as little peach pillows.

As I edit this chapter of my book, the people of Australia are in the news, suffering the worst forest fires in their history. People have died and thousands of homes have been lost. The cost to wildlife is unfathomable. We have been mercifully free from forest fires here this year, but they have reached Gabian in the past. Our friends, Hugh and Bassie, were evacuated with their three dogs when the *garrigue*[2] that surrounds them went up in flames. Driving back from Béziers, we are reminded again how threatening fires can be. We watch water-carrying planes, the Canadairs, on their way to put out a forest fire. The planes collect water from lakes, *étangs*, and any local water source. We see three going to and from the site of the fire.

We returned to England. We went with Maz and Johnny to surprise some friends holding a hundredth birthday party. Oh it was wonderful to see them all, and their dear, remembered faces smiling at us with pleasure. And the following day, Gazzie golfed and I wandered through Whitstable with Maz in hot autumn sunshine. Bliss.

At a party organised especially for us and our friends, we sat

---

1 Baked with a cheesy crust
2 Dry Mediterranean scrubland

on the beach as we have done in the past, and watched a Whitstable sunset. Beloved of so many painters, it is my belief they are the best sunset shows on earth.

We went to spend time with our daughter and family, and to visit our granddaughter, Bethany, in her new home. All this in four days, and only a two hour flight away! Return flights for two at €60, car hire at €35. Cheap as chips.

We're home in Gabian. We clean and polish and perfume the house in preparation for the first time visit of Lucie, an old friend from Suffolk, and a bit of a wine aficionado and gastronome. We take her to Saint-Chinian to taste their wines and to Les Fleurs at Olargues to taste the food. Lucie had offered to take us to Octopus in Béziers, awardee of a Michelin star, but I espied pig's ear on the online menu and decided it was a star too far for my naive palate.

On the journey up into the hills towards Olargues, we were discussing the Maquis, the French Resistance fighters, and imagining them hiding in the thickly wooded hillsides. While we were walking around this dear little village, Lucie discovered a small area, beside the river, dedicated to those brave men and women. It was deeply moving to stand in the quiet of this unchanging scenery and remember them. *Place of remembrance and contemplation. Pass through here often for they died for your freedom.* A very simple sign remembering those who fought for the freedom of France.

Then, as if to remind us of the men, women and animals who hid in the hills above us, with not a trodden leaf to announce its presence, I became aware, through the trees, of a grey horse silently watching our contemplations. And, as the shadows of the past slipped beyond our grasp, we moved back into the gentle afternoon of the present.

Pézenas, the town that never stops giving, last week had not

134

just its weekly market but a Grand Bazaar. This meant all the shops having massive sales, a loud but tuneful pipe and drum band, and a man talking excitedly into a microphone. It was innocent, it was fun, and it was charming.

I was engrossed in taking photos of the colourful vegetables, fruit, baskets and clothes when a weird thing happened.

'You won't believe this,' says Gazzie. 'There goes Dave from Whitstable.'

So we ran after him for cuddles and chats. When I went through the photos, I had photographed him coming out of a shop!

That day fed every one of the senses and left us emotionally exhausted, yet we ventured out on the morrow to see the new sculptures in Neffiès, the prettiest village of them all. And alongside the very modern art, as if from time immemorial the men, and now some women, played *boules*.

I am beginning to wonder if this village is actually a fantasy, like a French *Brigadoon*. On our way to see the church, every single person we passed smiled and said, '*Bonjour.*'[3] We stood quietly admiring the lovely building when, into a patch of sunlight in front of us, came a mother and two little girls who were holding hands and singing on their way home from nursery school.

Collective intake of breath and holding back of tears.

All is as it should be.

---

3 Good day

37

Tomorrow, just you wait and see

November 2018

And so, dear readers, to recap. That silver-tongued Lothario, also known as Gazzie, has talked me into spending another year in Languedoc.

As this first year was coming towards the end, I weighed up very carefully all the pros and cons of this new life and in the end it was not the beautiful scenery; nor the weather, which is often too hot for me; nor the amazing, warm and wonderful people we have met, – but me! Yes. It's about what the move has done for Me. I have become more interested in things and a little more adventurous, though still scared of dogs and walking. I have joined groups, learned some French, started a story and written my blog. I feel years younger. In my mind, at least. The adventure continues.

We take up our story *en route*[1] from our new home in Gabian, as of six days ago, to our house in Whitstable. We'll be staying for a week to reinstate the furniture for new tenants. Mistress R. Soul, Gaz and I are all going to have checkups: full service for her and the same for us. Having packed six suitcases and ten large bin bags of mainly my clothes, to move to the French house, we set about repacking for our trip home. I am determined to dispense with at least half my clothes before we move again. Promise . . .

On Tuesday 30th October, we set off with some trepidation because the previous day had seen heavy falls of snow throughout southern France. Our route was going to take us across the Massif Central which reaches an altitude of 1121 metres at its zenith. The Bear Grylls of the five star hotel world, our Gaz, filled the car with spades, boots, thermos flasks, Yeti deterrent. Everything needed for the intrepid explorer in a Kia Soul.

The motorway had been cleared but the countryside around us was thick with snow. Larch and Spruce tried manfully to lift their branches against the heavy burden. Gazzie was forced to wear sunglasses to protect his eyes against the white blaze. We travelled along amazing bridges – the red Eiffel Bridge and the now familiar Millau Viaduct, gunmetal grey against the bright blue sky.

It took us over four hours to drive across this high plateau. We experienced most weather conditions, save a sandstorm, and truly diverse terrain from stark limestone mountains to verdant plains. Cattle grazed and goats did whatever goats do. Horses chomped and sheep did too. They seem to favour white animals in these parts. Must make it difficult to find them in the snow. Or maybe they were covered in snow? Who can say? After hours driving beside the whiteout, our eyes were like wrinkled raisins in a dumpling. Gazzie's hands on the wheel, blue-fingered and white-knuckled, trembled as he pulled onto the verge in order

---

1 on the way

to leaf through *Scouting for Boys* in case there was a hurricane round the next bend.

The A75 took us gently down from the meteorological maelstrom of that amazing mountain range with its hardy inhabitants of one-house hamlets into the familiar territory of vineyards, wheat fields, lavender fields and other eye level stuff. Our necks creaked back into place and we prepared, after a light lunch, for the three hour journey to our resting place of Blois on the River Loire. We checked into our very reasonably priced hotel. It was nice.

Then a stroll into town. And food, *bien sûr*, of course. Braving the drizzle and darkening skies we wandered like two innocent children through the old streets, the shopping area and, ah ha, the restaurant area. Which to choose?

Why in the name of all that's holy did we pick the one we did? Well, it looked alright in the dark. Although it still looked Chinese. We had the worst food of any country in our entire lives: totally scallop-less scallop fritters, king prawns so overcooked the flesh refused to leave the shell, and enough garlic, I mean bricks of it, to do more damage to the digestive system than E.coli. Did we complain? Did we ask for our money back? No. We smiled Britishly, mumbled, 'Lovely,' and sat back to enjoy the beautifully chilled bottle of Vouvray for which the one-and-only waiter had mistakenly charged us €14. Fair dos, we thought. We were the only seated customers all evening and watched a parade of very strange, apparently non-paying customers come in and whisper to the waiter. He, a few minutes later, took small parcels over to the *salon du thé*[2] opposite. Early Christmas gifts no doubt.

The following day, after a lovely breakfast in the elegant dining room of our hotel of faded glory, we set out to explore Blois in the daylight. Blois is a beautiful city. Are there more

2 Tearoom

very old and beautiful cities in France than anywhere else in the world? Maybe we are under-travelled, but there seem to be.

In the grounds of the very impressive *Mairie* was a very butch statue of my heroine, Joan of Arc. I so wanted to be her when I was a young gal. And, you'll not be surprised to learn, I'm afraid of horses. And soldiers. And priests. And conflict. Still, I was young.

There was an exhibition by cartoonists from all over the world in support of Freedom of Expression and Peace. I was very moved. I asked myself, if so many of us so fervently desire such simple things, why can they not be achieved?

Then we saw a red metal reindeer, looking over the battlements. For Santa? God, I'm obsessed with that man, erm woman (trying for political correctness).

On this subject, with which I seem to be obsessed, my dear younger readers (the ones with the benefit of memory) will know I was a little disappointed last year to see so few Christmas decorations. I think I've sussed it. The decorations are put up at the beginning of October and by the end of December they have either been weather-ravaged or vandalised. The elegant bridge across the Loire had little red balls on all the lamp posts, which, I am sure, are illuminated at night.

We loved this place and spent too long admiring it, for ahead we had a four-hour journey to our next stop in Le Touquet. Eschewing (I love that word, but where does it come from?) the motorways for scenery for the soul and for Mistress Soul, we took the six hour non-motorway version. This took eight hours because we missed so many turnings whilst enjoying the bloody scenery.

Arriving at the Red Fox Hotel we were less like two innocent children and more like two old lags recently released from prison.

The thought of a glass of *vino*[3] revived us somewhat, despite the realisation that Halloween is a big night in France. Le Touquet was packed to the rafters. Many shops close the following day. I hope that the women who were screaming with laughter outside our hotel at four this morning worked in one that wasn't.

We know Le Touquet very well, having holidayed there on numerous occasions, but not for maybe ten years. Gosh, it has changed with lots of upmarket bars and lovely restaurants to attract those who've rambled through the pine forests during the day (you know me, I love a ramble). Very upbeat with many pedestrianised streets, I really want to go back again.

And for us old romantics, we found that our favourite restaurant, Café des Arts, was still open after thirty odd years, with the same two ladies waiting at table. And the most beautiful food. Lovely hotel too. Altogether a wonderful experience.

And now we are sitting in a tin box under the Channel. Only a three and a half hour wait to board.

We've arrived.

England, *mon amour!*[4]

---

3 Wine
4 My love

38

It's a long, long way

November 2018

We are on our way back to France after a trip to England to reinstate the furniture in our Whitstable home for new tenants. Mistress R. Soul has had a very expensive service. We have too. Much cheaper, ours, thanks to our National Health System.

While there, we caught up with friends and family. Ten of us met one evening to share food and wine. I felt a sweet contentment as our animated conversation was punctuated by smiles and laughter and shared memories. We revisited Wheelers restaurant in Whitstable, a favourite of ours over the last twenty years. Chef Mark is a magician of fish cuisine. Long may he welcome visitors from all over the world to his small and unpretentious establishment.

But back on the road, and wanting to avoid the meteorological vagaries of the Massif Central, we drove down the eastern side of France along the Autoroute des Anglais which becomes the Autoroute du Soleil. A much easier route, though less interesting. For our overnight stay, about halfway down, we chose Beaune, pronounced Bon by locals. It is the wine capital of Burgundy in the Côte-d'Or and is famous for the Burgundian tile, the polychrome Renaissance roofing style. The hospice structure in the town centre is one of the best preserved Renaissance buildings in Europe. The place has the feel of a university town with its little bars where students sit outside laughing, smoking and talking, despite the relentless rain.

We find a restaurant at the more reasonable end of the price range. Le Fleury. I choose two local dishes: *oeufs en meurette* (poached eggs in red wine, bacon and mushroom sauce) followed by *boeuf bourguignon*. Gazzie has snails in garlic followed by a Charolais beef steak. We share a bottle of the local white, very dry with a hint of honey. Yummy scrummy – a gastronomic term, mes amis, with which you may not be familiar. The following morning, we stroll the sunlit streets and wander back to the hotel to head back to Gabian.

Unfortunately, Mistress R. Soul, despite all the money spent on her, decides to down tools and refuses to start. The helpful hotel lady calls a car medic who kindly offers to jump the Mistress for €100! After two minutes' work, he sends us on our way with the warning: 'Whatever you do, don't stop.' A very tense four and a half hours later, I extricate Gazzie's paralysed fingers from the wheel. Our dear friends, Bassie and Hugh, feed, water and succour us. Back in the car, that damned contrary Mistress starts first time.

It was the 10th November 2018 when we crossed the Channel, the day before Remembrance Sunday, and at eight in the morning the tunnel was full with British families coming to France to commemorate with French families, the hundred-year anniversary of the end of World War I. Heavy rain was appropriately cleansing as we drove alongside the green pastures that now cover the battlefields of the Somme. The natural glory of autumn on both sides of the Channel paid fitting tribute to those men and women who gave their lives for our freedom.

A GARDEN
(Written after the Civil Wars)

SEE how the flowers, as at parade,
Under their colours stand displayed:
Each regiment in order grows,
That of the tulip, pink, and rose.
But when the vigilant patrol
Of stars walks round about the pole,
Their leaves, that to the stalks are curl'd,
Seem to their staves the ensigns furl'd.
Then in some flower's belovèd hut
Each bee, as sentinel, is shut,
And sleeps so too; but if once stirr'd,
She runs you through, nor asks the word.
O thou, that dear and happy Isle,
The garden of the world erewhile,
Thou Paradise of the four seas
Which Heaven planted us to please,
But, to exclude the world, did guard
With wat'ry if not flaming sword;
What luckless apple did we taste
To make us mortal and thee waste!
Unhappy! shall we never more
That sweet militia restore,
When gardens only had their towers,
And all the garrisons were flowers;
When roses only arms might bear,

And men did rosy garlands wear?
(Andrew Marvell 1621-1678)

When will we ever learn?
When will we ever learn?
(Pete Seeger 1955)

39

Wherever I lay my hat, that's my home

December 2018

After our trip to the UK at the beginning of November, we gathered our new home around us and wriggled to make it fit. Am I too old for so much wriggling? So much *new*?

The new house brings back old feelings of homesickness. I ache for the familiarity of Englishness. Here, the expensive heating and unreliable internet connection cause me frustration. We have moved into the very centre of the village where narrow streets meet and what I imagined would feel safe, feels claustrophobic. And Gary is part of the strangeness. He has become totally French in that he shrugs his shoulders and says, *'pffff'* to any problem that comes along. *Sang-froid*[1] personified.

But I do keep trying, dear readers. I really do. I've put flower boxes on the verandah and have Christmas trees and lights. It's beginning to look a bit like a home. Just not quite my home.

To all potential *émigrés*[2] I say, 'Don't believe everything you hear about the weather.' Winters can be very cold. As far as I can tell, the people of southern France believe their own fantasy that the weather is always temperate, because they do not heat their houses. I have been colder here than anywhere I've lived. Heating is either non-existent or exorbitantly expensive. Eskimos would be happy living in my house. In fact I am not absolutely sure there isn't a family of them living in our *cave*[3]. I might pop down and borrow some whale blubber.

But we did venture out for something festive because you do weird things when a drop of rain knocks out your TV signal. We had seen an advertisement for a Thanksgiving dinner to be held in one of the many uninhabited local chateaux. Leaving behind our mute and eyeless television screen, we headed out to the venue, whose name has fortunately been expunged from my memory. Hundreds of other people must have also lost their TV signal because there they were, huddled together like a colony of penguins crowded together for warmth. Now, if our American cousins choose this menu to celebrate the Pilgrim Fathers sharing a meal with the Native Americans, that is their business, but I'll not be joining the celebration again. I thought the only use for a pumpkin was as a Halloween decoration, and I was right. That is what they should be kept for. The pumpkin pie had the appearance of neon orange sludge – a waste of the pastry in

---

1 Composure/coolness
2 A person who has emigrated
3 Cellar

which it squelched. Turkey and sweet potato – no, no, no. Turkey needs fluffy, crispy roast potatoes to give its life (and death) some meaning. There needs to be roaring log fires, intimate surroundings, the happy, ruddy faces of friends and family, not the blue fingers and pinched expressions of one hundred and fifty strangers eating in mittens and mufflers. It was wrong, all wrong. For what were we giving thanks? For my part it was the knowledge that forevermore I will stick to a British Christmas dinner, with all its pitfalls, instead of eating the uneatable in an aeroplane hangar in northern Siberia.

Of course, my darlings, I couldn't keep up the misery forever and we quickly got into the swing of winter celebrations – Christmas Fairs in beautiful abbeys and chateaux and village squares, and concerts in churches and carol singing at markets. And why oh why did I think that the French in this area were hopeless at Christmas decorations? I don't know. Perhaps those in charge read my derogatory comments on last year's efforts and decided to prove me wrong. They most certainly have. Gaz and I went to Montpellier last week. What absolute joy. Though the temperature was around 22°C and there were blue skies, the atmosphere was giggly tummy Christmassy. There was an amazing Christmas market with everything to excite both adults and children with unique and beautiful decorations right across the town. After four hours of walking through both the old and newish town areas, a light Korean lunch (I know, I know. No wine though) we had still not seen all that the town had to offer. A really lovely day. Not one Christmas present bought but oh the people-watching. We, of the International People-Watching Brigade, found our Nirvana in France.

It was obviously a busy baby delivery day too because as we drove home, dozens of storks took rest from their labours on the just-lit street lamps.

147

And in the past few weeks the vines – nature's timepiece in these parts – have gone from a can-can of glorious colour to the last pirouette of a sole remaining leaf.

A couple of days later, we visited the most beautiful olive *domaine*: Pradines le Bas at Corneilhan, just outside Béziers. I would not have believed that so many different tastes could emerge from olive oil. A charming young woman, Corinne, knew all there was to know on the subject and Gaz and I spent a happy hour there. The owner was an avid art collector. The grounds were scattered with unusual sculptures and above the olive press was an impressive art gallery.

In a week's time, we will have been here for a year. We celebrated with a beef and stout lunch at the Sarabande vineyard, scene of so many happy summer evenings. The grapes we picked in the summer have been barrelled and sold. So much hard work for this young couple. They not only produce wine, but experiment with beer, gin, port and absinthe, all palatable, some exceptionally so. Like *vignerons* of old, they use the land and their crop to be financially independent and to keep their family safe, warm and well fed.

Capturing the spirit of the coming Christmas season, Bassie (you know her – she's the one who started us on this grand and perilous adventure) is very, very busy. She and her friends belong to Languedoc Solidarity with Refugees (LSR) and are working every moment possible to provide a Christmas party for local refugee children. In 2014, there was a meeting in the village hall in Roujan to discuss the plight of sixteen Syrian families who were found squatting in Béziers. They decided to help them, at first by providing food. Call-outs were sent on social media and food rolled in. To fulfil legal obligations, it was necessary to form a proper association to handle the finances. Gary and Windela Kilmer and other volunteers set up the Conseil d'Administration.

The aim of this multicultural group is to provide humanitarian support and to increase awareness of the refugee crisis in Languedoc. They raise money from direct donations and charity events and collect food donations for their food banks which help refugee families settling in the area. Furniture and household goods are collected and stored to donate to families once they are homed.

One of their most time-intensive events is that Christmas party. Volunteers buy, wrap and personally label two or three gifts each for Père Noël to give to seventy refugee children, paid for with funds from donations. Professional entertainment is laid on and refugee parents provide much of the food. It is a truly happy occasion when families can forget for a few hours the horror of the risks they took to get here. And for those who work to help them, and those of us who admire the work they do, and you too probably, dear readers, we give thanks for our opportunities and our safety.

You may be aware of the massive surge of dissatisfaction in France with protestors known as the *Gilets Jaunes*, Yellow Vests, taking to the streets and preventing the free flow of traffic. We have suffered nothing compared with Paris but they have stationed themselves on the roundabout to our local supermarket for three weeks now. They slow down the traffic and have blocked some supermarket deliveries, but are generally polite and smiley. This weekend they have stepped up the civil disobedience and are barricading airports. We fervently hope this won't prevent us from going home for Christmas in two weeks' time.

Shall I continue this memoir in the New Year? If next year proves as exciting and life-affirming as this one, then maybe . . . once in a while . . .

'Merry Christmas to us all, God Bless us, everyone,' said one small, sickly Dickens character. Jumbo Jan and Gorgeous Gaz say, 'We wish you all a happy, healthy and hopeful New Year.'

40

Someday soon we all may be together

January 2019

We had booked our flight home for Christmas and like two kids going to visit Father Christmas in Lapland, we trembled with excitement as we got in the car, all packed and painted for the holibobs. Checking his phone for emails, Gary said a very rude word.

'Cancelled,' he said. 'The flight's cancelled. Something about drones.'

We went back indoors. We looked for another flight. The email was three hours old, so flights were either full or ridiculously expensive. I pictured the disappointed faces of our children and grandchildren, curly-haired innocents looking spookily similar to those cherubic children in *It's a Wonderful Life*.

'Oh, Husband,' said I. 'We cannot let the faaaamily down. We have to get there somehow.' A crystal tear fell attractively down my cheek.

Being now experienced bad weather travellers after our recent drive over the Massif Central, Bear Grylls (five star hotel branch) got together rope, spades, vacuum flasks, space blankets, mountain boots. He gathered us all up and strapped us in. As an aside, he's also known as Bare Thrills, but you may prefer not to know that. Or was it Bare Frills?

Bare donned his Davy Crockett hat and we were off.

'We'll have to do motorways, Wife,' says Bare.

'Oh no, Husband,' says Wife.

'Desperate times, old fruit,' he says.

Wife smiles. Though her eyes tell a different story.

And so my hero drove. We left Gabian at 8.30 am and fighting juggernauts, indicator-less drivers, rain and eye level sun, we came within two hours of Calais where we took the big risk of booking the 9.40 pm tunnel crossing. The crossing was late so we just made it.

Euphoria hit us when we arrived in Folkestone. We had to cancel a planned dinner and overnight stay with *Les Fromages* and asked our daughter if we could stay with her in Maidstone. We kept her informed of progress and when we arrived in Ashford to find the M20 closed, euphoria disappeared quicker than Communion wine at Midnight Mass. We texted daughter to tell her we'd be there in about thirty minutes. A regretful text gave the reply that, as they'd had a long day, they were off to bed and would leave the door on the latch. We understood. Sort of.

At 10.20 pm (British time) we turned into our daughter's drive, fifteen hours after leaving home. And suddenly her house was flooded with Christmas lights, carols filled the air and the next-door neighbours merrily called out, 'Turn that bloody lot off or we'll call the police.' Daughter and husband, dressed as

Father Christmasses, were there with open arms, mulled wine, sausage rolls and mince pies. And we were James Stewart's wide-eyed, curly children.

'Just like the Waltons,' I sighed to daughter.

'More like the Griswolds,' she replied.

Our plans for the week at home had to be adjusted but we managed to get round for quick cuddles with most friends and relatives, a great Games Evening and lovely welcome home meals, then back to our daughter's for Christmas festivities. So much fun, food and wine, my body began to groan for mercy. But we're British, we do not flag. We kept on with the imbibements.

Boxing Day found us striding through country lanes. Well, not exactly striding, maybe sidling. Whilst others, with dogs, did a ninety minute ramble across fields like real country folk, we did a more sedate, less stridey walk along country lanes. However, we did refuse several offers of lifts from merry Christmas strangers. Followed by more food and the bliss of being with old friends.

And soon enough it was time for very tearful goodbyes. Sara, shivering in her pyjamas, waved us off at 6.00 am as Bare and I set off, once again, for Folkestone and Le Shuttle. Good time to travel. Straight on the train and before long, we were *oui*-ing and *non*-ing again.

We had decided to avoid the stress of the motorway and go cross-country. Stunning scenery spread before us. We enjoyed thick frost on field and tree, tiny hamlets twinkling with fairy lights, empty roads and cold turkey sandwiches. Joy to the King. And to us.

As evening cast its long grey fingers across the landscape, and Gary's eyes began to ache, we pulled into an *aire*[1] to look at maps and decide whether to look for shelter or press on.

What was the pull to press on? I don't know. The desire to

---

1 Motorway rest-stop

be home perhaps, however temporary that home may be? I left the final decision with the driver and, in accord, we headed for the motorway.

I will say here that Gary's stamina is phenomenal. He may, on occasion, present his funny, rather soft side, but when the chips are down he can be depended upon to eat them off the floor. Not once did he make me feel guilty for not sharing the driving. He didn't swear, didn't moan and just got on with the job in hand. We sang carols, made up silly words to favourite songs, and the time crept on. We did battle with heavy rain, lorries overtaking and deluging us, accidents and terrifyingly thick fog. Sometimes we drove in silence. And the time crept on.

Finally we reached the *péage*² off the motorway at Florensac/Sainte-Thibéry which had been closed by *Gilets Jaunes* on the way up. There was one faint green light showing and behind it a huge bonfire warming half a dozen protestors. With sinking hearts, we drove slowly towards the barrier. It raised its ghostly arm and we drove through without paying. The *Gilets* waved wearily as we passed them. Our stoicism suddenly crumbled. We had been on the road for nearly nineteen hours and progress during the last thirty minutes was slightly weepy, slightly beaten, rather slow.

At 12.40 am we fell in the door, took out the dustbin, and slept.

The following day we started preparations for our New Year's Eve dinner party for eleven friends. The menu had been planned, other friends were bringing starters and desserts, and we had ordered two kilos of meat to make venison, chestnut and mushroom in Madeira sauce.

Oh, very happy days! We ate like kings, drank like, um . . .

---

2 Motorway pay booth

drinky people, played the old games like Charades and Consequences, and before we knew it, it was five to twelve. No Jools Holland for us, we're an hour ahead, so a French person on the radio led us into 2019. We'll have an hour longer than you then, this year. Every one of us oldies made it to midnight, many of us for the first time in many years.

That first day of the New Year we walked around our new village, feeling the ancient stones and our insignificance compared with the lives seen by them over the last six hundred years. Street signs in French and Catalan reminded us that this area has been both French and Spanish and yet, in our local bar, we are known by our names, not by our country of birth.

Happy New Year to friends old and new. And to you dear readers. Bring on *l'année nouvelle*[3].

Come, take my hand, let's see what we shall see . . .

41

Cage aux folles

March 2019

The bedroom window is a skylight. We open the blind each morning to see the colour of the sky. It is mostly blue.

The days rush by like a speeded up movie. Since the action-packed adventure of our Christmas trip home, we've done more travelling around, more meals out, movies, reading, writing, quiet times and busy times, and special times.

At the end of December, our friends Mandy and JC with Kicker Dog arrived for a six week stay in the area. They became immersed in the French way of life, at least of the medical kind, with visits to doctors, dentists and vets to find cures for their numerous health problems. After a few days with us, they moved to their rental property in Magalas. Their British landlord was unhelpful and a disgrace to the rental community. He hadn't done a thing to get the place ready. It took four of us thirty minutes to get into the house to be greeted by cobwebs, dirt and leaves everywhere, mouse-chewed bed linen (where there was any), moulding food in the oven, and exorbitantly costly heating. Son of Rachman, however, had not counted on the masterful and determined Mrs Collins. Her email tongue sent paper cuts over the ether and eventually, and at a cost, she and John managed to have a reasonably happy stay. We had lots of lovely, cosy evenings, eating together and playing cards, and they did lots of beautiful touristy stuff.

The beginning of February brought our daughter Sara, her friend Georgia, and the loving, funny teddy bear that is Harley the Cavapoodle. You notice I avoided the word dog. There, I've said it. But Harley shared few of the traits of the animals I fear: barking, smelling, licking their bits and then human faces. Unfortunately he did need frequent W things. I declined to take part, you will not be surprised to learn.

Sara had booked the same villa as Mandy but they stayed with us first for a fortnight while we planned how to make the most of their stay: intensive French lessons in Béziers, gym membership and aquaswim membership in Magalas, yoga lessons, wine tastings in local *domaines*, trying local restaurants, and going to places of interest. Gaz and I were fatigued just listening to it all. Finally it was time for them to take over ex-Mandy-house. Mandy and John, bless them, had ironed out most of the difficulties and after completely rearranging the furniture, lighting the log burner and with the local wine in the fridge, the girls pronounced themselves well and truly *chez nous*[1].

I have written of Roquebrun before, a beautiful hillside town renowned for water sports. Heralding the spring, this little town puts on a festival to celebrate the mimosa which grows

---

1 At home

abundantly in the area. It was worth the one mile walk from the parking area: stalls selling wine, honey, cheese, lavender, olive oil, fruit and, to feed the hungry, barbecued boar and chips, paella, hamburgers and churros. We needed the long walk back to recover. But the main attraction was the flowering trees that grow abundantly in this town. The whole village was bathed in yellow. It was blossoming on the trees in the village, up in the Mediterranean Garden, and was for sale in huge bunches which we took home to bring spring into our homes.

We had long planned to drive the girls to Sitges in Spain, for the Mardi Gras Carnival. The four of us, plus Bassie and Harley the Cavapoo, set off in high excitement, our carnival costumes packed, and arrived at the amazing apartment close to the centre of town. That first evening, the parade was a family-oriented panoply of colour and noise, taking two hours to pass beneath the hotel balcony where we were watching. Walking back to our apartment also took hours because the watching crowds blocked the pavement and highway.

It was only on arrival that Gary realised that his phone and credit card had been stolen. We went through the usual, 'Didn't I give them to you to look after?' and, 'When did we last use them?' We had never had anything stolen before so the experience felt unreal, but we cancelled the credit card online and saw that already there had been two failed attempts to use it. Gary also did something clever on the internet which locked the phone, preventing further use. It certainly taught us a lesson about carrying phones and credit cards in an unzipped rucksack in crowded streets, but quick action had prevented any serious repercussions and resulted in only a small inconvenience.

The second evening was the Pride Parade. We had never seen anything quite like it. Not in our whole lives. Apart from Gary, we were dressed in shocking pink tutus and wigs, but even so we were like little brown sparrows compared to the thousand peacocks who surrounded us. Delicious costumes worn by six foot, muscly men in five inch heels would have outshone many a West End musical. And some of those costumes were very, very naughty. I averted my eyes, naturally, but it was difficult not to look when those Carnival Queens were sitting beside us, parading in front us and asking to be photographed, questioned, appreciated. The freedom-to-be was infectious. The atmosphere inclusive. And yet when I could drag (see what I did there?) my eyes away from the particular, and viewed the scene from above, it was like a Dalí-esque painting, giddy with frenetic movement and colour. Before the night became wilder still, we regretfully took our leave and wandered back to the apartment, our eyes wide with wonder.

Sitges, after the madness had gone to bed and the street cleaners had washed away the night's excesses, awoke restored as a beautiful seaside town. The streets were wet and slick, clean white linen clothed last night's tables, the sea glittered blue and silver and the naked faces of last night's revellers were innocent as lambs as we set off for a four mile walk around the coast. Exquisite – not a word I often use in conjunction with walking – but the sparkly sea on our right and the whitewashed buildings to our left, even with the purgatory of a long walk, suited the adjective and matched our morning mood of regeneration.

We took advantage of Spain's much lower prices in the local shops and at the border, then journeyed home quietly, empty of fun, speech, money and the ability to move our limbs. Apart from Harley, who was remarkably chipper after all the festivities.

Back on home territory, with *Les Fromages* revisiting, we returned to Sète. I feel I should adjust my views on this place. I have previously said that I do not like it, being too big and too grubby for me. Because our new visitors wanted to visit the Paul Valéry Museum, we drove high above the town to the site of the museum and the old and rather beautiful cemetery whose ornate memorial stones are enhanced by the backdrop of the sea. From the nearby observation point you get a bird's-eye view of the town, its waterways and avenues, and its attraction became more obvious. On a very sunny March day it looked almost inviting.

And so, dear readers, we've had more goodbyes and more welcomes. We meet new and interesting people, visit new and familiar places in a winter that has been unseasonably warm . . . and yet I have days of longing for the grey skies of England.

And those grey skies seem to be indicative of a United Kingdom that is fatally divided, its politicians unable to lead the country, its parliamentary procedure tossed aside to suit those wrangling for power while the people remain powerless. A country once proud of its democratic values is now a laughing stock to the whole of Europe, and possibly the world. Whether we leave the European Union or stay, it will take a very long time for the British people to learn to trust again in our democratic process.

42

Starry starry night

April 2019

England, our homeland, is neither in Europe, nor out of Europe. We are in La La Land.

We continue our hedonistic lifestyle, though in reality we spend many days houseworking, shopping, reading and trying to get the damned television to give us a few English programmes. Or any programmes at all. It is my view that President Macron, unaware of our total powerlessness, is purposely blocking our signal so that we'll go home and force Britain to Remain.

We would, however, be foolish to stay indoors all the time

and not take advantage of the beautiful and varied countryside that is within a short drive (or, God forbid, walk) of our rented home. Winters are, generally, milder here and there are many early-year-days when the weather is warm enough to walk without coats, or preferably to sit outside enjoying the views and having a small glass of the local wine.

In the UK, to plan a carnival with a street parade in early April would be risky. Not so here. The residents of the seaside village of Bouzigues were confident that their parade would go ahead. And so it did. It was a tenth of the size of the one in Sitges with only four floats but the enthusiasm of the participants was every bit as, if not more, infectious. It was also all inclusive, in that we were side by side with those who had spent many hours rehearsing and many days decorating their floats. We felt totally at one with everyone there. At times we forgot we should be just watching, and took part.

In mid-April came our first visits to the pop-up beach clubs, or *paillottes*, or *guingettes*, the temporary beach clubs, rebuilt each year, where we can hire wonderfully comfortable sunbeds and have reasonably priced lunches. With visiting children and grandchildren, friends and their families, we happily bathed in the sunshine and in the sea, before travelling home, sandy and sun-bronzed, sizzling with vitamin D and bonhomie.

I am very pleased to say that our daughter, Sara, has also fallen in love with Languedoc. During her three month stay, she learnt some French (mostly yoga instruction) and introduced us to places she had found. One of these was the Lerab Ling Buddhist Temple at Roqueredonde, deep in the countryside, near Lodève. To come upon this exotic building, set deep among the green woods and shaven hills of France was a surreal experience. We drove through thickly wooded countryside, with the dappled sun occasionally illuminating tantalising spots of gold, then suddenly, at a bend in the road, we saw the temple, its turrets and gleaming cupola. We parked and walked the long flag-lined path to the heavily embossed temple door and the lake beside it on which the golden statues of the Buddhist gods appeared to float. There was not a living soul to be seen as we walked back past the simple cottages where visitors stay whilst attending the courses run by the monks. There was a sense of peace and we vowed to return on one of their Open Days.

In Whitstable, one of my greatest joys is our monthly, rather radical, Not-the-Book-Club meetings. So much did I miss them that I've started one here called Book Club Plus in which, over lunch, we discuss a favourite book from the past or present. The range of literature is huge, from Colette to Ian McEwan. Food, friends, books and conversation. What a combination!

As I have said before, our friend, Bassie, is the networker *extraordinaire* behind many of our new meetings and new events. Last week, we went for lunch at Maman Des Poissons (Fish Mother) in Pézenas, a tapas bar with good food and very friendly service. There, Bassie and I, with Tricia from the Book Group, met Lynn Michell, a published author with a small book publishing business. My goodness. Other people's lives! Lynn lives up in the hills in a house she and her husband have hewn out of the rocks. Her husband is an academic as well as a builder of houses and they chose to follow their separate careers here in Languedoc. I look forward to learning more about her life as we, together with another friend, get together once a fortnight to do some creative writing, with Lynn's guidance. Incidentally, Tricia, another creative writer, is an International Baccalaureate Educator and lectures on Pathways to Future Education. Just can't get away from teachers. And don't want to.

We have wanted to visit Arles since arriving here. Only about an hour and a half away, it is easily achievable in a day, but our dislike of motorways combined with the proximity of Arles to Aix-en-Provence made this a two day trip.

You have already witnessed how the diva that is Mistress R. Soul combined with Miles the Satnav's inability to read maps have made us miss, or be very late for dozens of events. 'Here we go again,' we thought, separately, as we circled Aix for two hours trying to reach our hotel. We had chosen the day of the Iron Man race. Every route into town was *barrée*[1]. We stopped in a parking space to assess the situation and to try to find a possible route when an apparently friendly resident knocked on the car door. Like the trusting innocents that we are, we wound down the window. By gesticulation and the odd understood word, he seemed to be telling us that our registration plate had been scanned by security cameras and we would be fined €100 if we didn't immediately pay for parking at the meter on the next corner.

'I'll come with you to show you,' said the helpful man.

Like a lamb to the slaughter, Gazzie got out and followed the kind soul who even offered to take the credit card and insert it in the machine. Tired and frustrated, he was nearly duped but held on to his card. I shudder to think what might have happened if he hadn't. No violence ensued and a relieved husband slipped back into the car, shaky but safe.

By going back on the motorway and taking a different route in, we found our hotel. Thereafter (actually Wineafter) Aix revealed itself to us in all its beauty. We dined in Les Deux Garçons, the oldest and most famous restaurant in the town, frequented in the past by the likes of Van Gogh, Cézanne and Jean Cocteau. Presumably they all died in poverty after paying the prices for food which tasted as if it had been cooked in the thirties, buried, and resurrected for our delectation. Oh, how we laughed as we paid the eye-watering bill.

---

1 Blocked

We were excited to find that Aix has a little tourist train. A favourite of ours, as you know by now, dear readers. Under the watchful gaze of Monsieur Cézanne, immortalised in bronze, we mounted the train and set off in bright sunshine to discover some of this famous Provençal city. The City of a Thousand Fountains is deservedly a tourist magnet and we were pleased we visited at the edge of the tourist season. We touristly wandered the ancient streets, craning our necks to look up at roof lines, which one only does when being touristy. Bizarre shop signs caught our eyes: Oh My Cream (beauty salon), Insane (dress shop) and WOMB (World Of My Baby).

After a light snack, we visited the famous Cathedral of St. Sauveur which was beautiful. What caught my eye was a statue of St. Therese Of The Roses, the title of a pop song sung by Malcolm Vaughan in 1956. I aim to educate as well as amuse. Whether I do either is not up for debate.

We set off in the afternoon for the hour-long journey to Arles. Gazzie had picked our hotel because of its proximity to the centre and the fact that it was film-themed. Cheaper than the hotel in Aix, this was my dream stay. Husband, unusually, done good.

Although we love little tourist trains, friends had told us that the Arles Tourist Tuk-Tuk was fun so we booked in advance and met Soufrian, our guide and driver, in Place de la République. We mounted. The tail end of the Mistral was rattling our tuk-tuck alarmingly but Soufrian peddled like a mouse on a wheel and squeezed between bollards of the exact width of our vehicle, while mouthing amazing information. Gazzie and I nodded encouragingly and knowingly, until, after a puzzling thirty minutes, we realised he wasn't talking about Cèzanne and Gauguin, but Caesar and Augustus! And thus we made our confused and shaking way through the narrow, pedestrianised streets of a French town whose Roman roots are beautifully preserved. How symbolic then that our fellow guests at the hotel, and always just ahead of us at the ancient tourist sites, was a Korean women's football team! Some things are changing for the better.

Between Aix and Arles, we approached what was to be the *pièce de résistance, la crème de la crème*[2] of our visit. Les Carrières de Lumières[3] at Les Baux. The white limestone used in local buildings has been dug from quarries since Roman times, forming huge caverns in which we found a world of wonder waiting for us. I had never even been to a *Son et Lumière*[4] before so I was totally unprepared. Having paid a reasonable entrance fee, you enter caves which are completely dark, except for projections, on the fifty foot high walls, the ceilings and floors, of Van Gogh paintings, moving across and over one another, each to the accompaniment of music of every genre. It is very difficult to explain the experience, but Gary and I agreed that it was a deeply spiritual one and like nothing we had ever seen or felt before. The exhibitions change annually. I can't wait to return. We drove back to our home in Gabian, through acres and acres of wild poppies, eyes and souls overflowing.

I am aware, as always, that I record the highlights of our life here and would not want to give the impression that our life is a series of events strung together on a chain of inertia. Because we are in a limbo land, between holiday and residence, we are tourists at the same time as residents who pay electricity and medical bills, and take the rubbish to the tip. But there is a disconnect. We don't vote here, don't pay taxes, are not fully cognisant of the political system. We struggle to read French newspapers and watch French television. So, freedom or

2 The very best
3 The Quarry of Lights.
4 Sound and light show

irresponsibility? Whatever it is, that's the way it will be until October, when we return home to reflect on our future.

That is the plan at the moment.

43

No, nobody's gonna rain on my parade

June 2019

Today, Pézenas had more rain in one hour than it should have had in a month, so we light the fire and I curl myself around the iPad and reflect on the past two years and their impact on me.

I admit that from my miserable, flu-stricken, homesick beginnings, I have become a bit of a hedonist, making the most of the winter years of my life. Here, I have found joy and laughter, the company of good friends, and as much excess as my old-age-pension and arthritis-plagued body will permit. It turns out to be quite a lot of excess. Of course, I could have found all of that in England but being in France has *allowed* me greater freedom, less need to conform, for what would I conform to? My lack of understanding of the customs and culture of my adopted country gives me an excuse not to conform, and kindness and respect will tide me over until I do. And our travels around the lovely Languedoc and further afield continue, somewhat curtailed, but not unabated because there is still so much to see.

On our arrival home from our visit to Aix and Arles, summer was knocking gently on the door. We opened the windows and shook out the winter mantle of dark and cold. We packed away our warm clothes, winter duvets and electric blankets. We uncovered swimming pools and cleaned verandahs that were decked with petunias. We got ready for outside living. Gosh, that was all jolly tiring, but necessary as I'm preparing for a mainly horizontal summer.

Soon we were heading back to the beach, last year's swimsuits tried on, then discarded in favour of full body burkas. There is no designated parking area at Vendres Plage and vehicles park haphazardly wherever they can find a space. We saw a gap between two cars and poked Mistress Soul's big red nose in as far as we could.

'Lucky finding that last space,' said Gazzie.

And so there we were, first week in May, lying on the beach, book in one hand and a glass of rosé in the other. Lush. Not lush in the alcoholic sense, but Welsh colloquial for wonderful. Why didn't I just say wonderful? Well, a bit of variety here and there, you know.

Sun-kissed and serene at the end of our day, we returned to Mistress S.

'Lovely day, darling,' says Husband, pressing his accelerator with a merry little tap. Mistress R. Soul was either being obstructive or we were stuck. Oh, it was that last thing. Stuck. We'd driven into a sand pit 'and them wheels they kept on turning . . . '. Various kind French people tried to push.

'*Poussez! Poussez!*'[1] But they pushed us further in.

A crowd of about twenty stood around offering French advice, scratching French heads and telling French children, 'Hush, Papa is trying to help stupid English man.' Until *Superhomme*[2], in the shape of a 'five foot and a fag paper' Frenchman in a very big 4x4, joined us to him with a very big rope and pulled us out, to the cheers of, now fifty, French people and their bored but relieved French children. I moan less about gas-guzzling-penis-extension drivers these days.

What with the shame, and having totted up the cost of eating and drinking at the increasingly more expensive *paillottes*, we have opted instead for lazy days at Gabian *Plage*[3] (aka Hugh and Bassie's gaffe). We take sandwiches and pop, read and dream, chat and scheme, and all for a fraction of the cost of the beach bars. And much closer to home.

June found us back in Sitges in Spain with *Les Fromages*. They too have fallen in love with Languedoc and the opportunities it offers for access to other parts of Europe. We returned to our favourite tapas bar, trawled the shops, and sea-dreamed a while. We stayed in an old and lovely hotel near the station which was handy, because we were going to Barcelona by train the next day. A grand adventure. The rail journey was easy and quick but as we emerged from the railway station, somebody in the great weather station in the sky opened the floodgates and we were virtually swimming upright as we fought our way through rainwater coming from every direction. The bits of us missed by water from the sky were caught by spray from the traffic.

---

1 Push

2 Superman

3 Beach

Of course, dear dry readers, we sought the comfort of a small café and waited it out with coffee and croissants. On the way, we passed the about-to-open Picasso exhibition.

'We'll call in there later,' we promised ourselves.

Forty-five minutes later hundreds of sodden people were queuing in the rain. We walked on.

Determined to see the Gaudí Cathedral, we stopped off in a shoe shop to replace our sodden shoes, then off we went again. Several hours later, four colourful, little figures (little because we'd all shrunk by this time) arrived with undisguised joy at . . . an underground station. We hopped, well squished really, onto the train and in no time stood before the amazing edifice which is La Sagrada Família. Señor Gaudí did a jolly fine job. The building was breathtaking. Even through the moisture-heavy clouds, we could see that each facade has intricate detail that intrigues the eye and stirs the soul. Dripping noisily on the floor of a nearby café, we steamed, and wordlessly paid homage.

This month also gave us a quick trip home to celebrate our daughter's silver wedding anniversary. Gosh, how I love being with my family and their loyal and steadfast friends. And with *our* loyal and steadfast friends with whom we shared a goodbye dinner on the beach at Whitstable. Gosh, all my darlings, you do make it so hard for me.

Of course, there was some trudging through the treacle of homesickness after that, for if we didn't miss parts of our former life, it would have no meaning and it certainly was important to us. But we have thrown ourselves happily back into our French ways. And so the summer days dreamed slowly on, with Gazzie playing golf and me meeting amazing women (and men, once in a while) on boat trips on the Canal du Midi, at the wonderful Sarabande Sundays, and in cafés and social gatherings all over Languedoc. Being the sensation seekers I now admit we are, we had to try the newly-opened restaurant in a crater formed by a meteor! Well, I tell you, my darlings, a Michelin-starred meal is not worth the half-hour descent over rock and shale and, worse still, the climb back in the dark.

One of the very special places where I've met some wonderful women is the book club I've told you about. So many books I've been introduced to and made friends with! A great group of people too. We each bring a plate of food and eat together afterwards when conversation grows wider and sometimes wilder.

And oh my goodness, how I love our creative writing group. Five of us meet once a fortnight for two hours to, well, create and share. The women are inspiring, companionable, trusting, life-enhancing and probably several other adjectives. Like all the best learning environments, the pupils love their time together. Three women are writing a form of memoir which involves a deep level of trust, and whilst offering our opinions, we are always aware that constructive comment should be tempered with respect. For, as old W. B. Yeats said, 'I have spread my dreams under your feet, tread softly, for you tread upon my dreams:'.

I'm not being curmudgeonly, I hope, when I say that as one gets older, birthdays only serve as reminders of one's mortality. Thank goodness, then, for friends who refuse to let me dwell on 'how much longer?' and insist on making the most of every minute. And so my birthday passed in a happy haze of hilariousness.

The day after, with excitement and anticipation, four of us set off in two separate cars for Roses in Spain. The weather was gorgeous and we spent the days on the beach opposite our hotel, and the evenings walking to some amazing restaurants, one of which will serve a chocolate-covered Foie Gras Magnum. Incredible. I'm told. The reason for the two cars was so we could buy a Spanish pot for my birthday tulip bulbs and some household products that cost half the price of their French counterparts. So, we actually saved money!

In the spirit of grabbing life by the *cojones*[4], we did a quick unpack, wash and iron, and three days later were back at Béziers airport to collect *Les Fromages*. Two days of wine acclimatisation later, we set off, brave voyagers, into the great unknown that is the west coast of France.

---

4 Literally, *testicles*, (colloquial) meaning courage or 'guts'

44

You can't draw here, Madame

November 2019

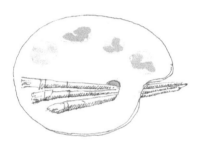

And so the September journey was planned. With *Les Fromages*, Maz and Johnny, we visited the *brocante* market in Béziers and then headed straight for our first stop: Périgeux.

Having checked in, we set off to explore this city famed for the Black Truffle. Having never tasted a truffle of any hue (save the chocolate kind) I was disappointed that they were not in season, but we managed to find some preserved ones and some oil which, unselfishly, we took as gifts to our daughter. So they remain unknown to me.

After a short overview walk we fell upon a most agreeable hostelry for some liquid refreshment. The Silver Owl is run by two hospitable and engaging fellows, Hank and Chris, with whom we spent a happy half-hour before setting off to eat in a restaurant they recommended and booked for us. A great gastronomic experience awaited us at Le Clos Saint Front. Beautiful food. Impeccable service. Thank you chaps!

Yet again we enjoyed acquainting ourselves with a city *en fête*[1] and looking very jolly. After visiting the cathedral, and coffee and croissanting, we decided to do something not beginning with C and jumped into Mistress R. to burn a few miles towards our next destination. As we were passing within a gnat's burp of La Rochelle, Someone (who shall be nameless but sometimes has red hair) said we should visit one of the isles off the coast. We eschewed the more popular Île de Ré in favour of Saint-Pierre-d'Oléron, because someone had told Someone that the latter was just like our home town of Whitstable in Kent. Hah. More like Alcatraz. Admittedly the rain was falling like a million knitting needles and we had to be tied together to prevent the wind scooping us up and placing us in the Outer Hebrides, but even so . . .

Whilst on the subject of torrential rain, dear readers, I have noticed that when *Les Fromages* are around, it is like living under the sea, so damp is the climate. The other day, as we were doing our third change into dry shoes, I couldn't help but see that their feet have a slightly webbed appearance. And, as if that was not evidence enough, whenever we're with them, we are followed by this biblical old bloke chanting, 'Two by two, now, two by two. Get your places on Noah's Ark.' I'm thinking of renting them out to a couple of the more arid areas of the world. For a long time.

As alcoholics to the bottle, we were drawn to the shelter of the one café open on the island and from the safety of its interior, we watched a couple walking, we presume, towards that ark. They seemed to be the only inhabitants. Perhaps everyone else was on board, ready to sail to safety. I think Miles Satnav had brought us to the island of Atlantis. During the Submerged Years.

We had been whipped by wind and soaked by storm, but continued onwards to seek the promised beauty. We were giddy

---

1 In the midst of celebration

with turning into wrong turnings, and driving into, and backing out of, cul-de-sacs. Then Mistress R. Soul stopped, locked her windscreen wipers and refused to move. We laughed. What else to do? We asked the advice of Miles Satnav but he was as lost as we were, so we resorted to an old-fashioned road map. Eventually Mistress R. got over her paddy and we went on our way, our stomachs aching with laughter.

Gazzie floored it to get to our next stop at Poitiers. Oh, favourite town (favourite actor too, Sidney). I don't really know why we all loved it so much. It was small enough to be explored in one day and everywhere was simply delightful. Our arrival had not been auspicious, which may not surprise you, the way this trip had been going so far. Bloody Booking Dot Con (as we now call it) had omitted to inform us that our card had not worked. Arriving at our hotel at 7.00 pm, we were told they had no room for us. Our jolliness evaporated and we sat wringing our hands while the very kind hotel receptionist searched for alternative accommodation. Half an hour later, she smiled and directed us to a matchbox in the centre of the city. Great location, slightly cramped accommodation. I had Johnny and Gary snoring in stereo. But I repeat, a wonderful location.

Chartres, famous for its cathedral, was our next stop. I thought a lot about religious architecture on this journey – there was a lot of it and of unrivalled splendour. Whatever our religious affiliation, some of these edifices stand alone as works of art. I tried not to think of the human sacrifice that raised them into glory and just admired the work of artist and artisan.

En route to Chartres, we drove through the Loire Valley, justifiably known for its natural and architectural glory. Along the way we stopped for a picnic off the motorway. I'm sure there was an idyllic setting nearby, but we didn't find it. We had neither cutlery nor bottle opener but found hitherto unknown uses for a credit card such as cutting cheese and spreading butter. Handy, especially as it's obviously no good for booking hotels.

Hardly had we set off again than we were screeching to a halt because we had spotted the sign for a Vouvray wine *domaine*. We spent a very happy hour there, dégusting and choosing. Our host was a doppelgänger for the Reverend Richard Coles and he kept us in fits of laughter with his tales of his vineyard.

B.B.Con struck again with our aparthotel in Chartres. We drove for five miles to pick up the key to a tobacco-infused apartment of shabby furniture, dirty crockery and a broken kettle. We made haste to get out and see the town, and enjoyed a very French Indian meal before seeking out the illumined buildings. Nor were we disappointed. No wonder *Son et Lumi◻re* is French; they are masters of the art. Trying to put off our return to our accommodation, the four of us illuminated ourselves with light up bow ties and tiaras. I think we had several admiring glances.

From the sublime to the not quite ridiculous, on the way out of Chartres we visited Maison Picassiette, an ordinary house in an ordinary street, except that the owner was obsessed with mosaics and had mosaic-ed everything: the cooking range, the sewing machine, the garden, the bed and possibly his wife too. Bet she had to hide the cup and saucer after a nice cuppa, fearing it might end up on the wall of the outside loo.

Can you have too much beauty? This day was destined to deliver beauty overload, for as we left this amazing house before we too were covered in bits of broken crockery, we set out, brave voyagers, for Giverny, home of the late M. Monet, who painted water lilies for the last thirty years of his life. Fortunately he did some other stuff too which we saw at the house. And he managed to do a bit of gardening and some jolly adventurous home decorating. I could have lived in that house, but deadheading in the garden might have defeated me. It was here, dearest readers, that young Marilyn Fromage, who likes a dabble herself, was told that she could not draw in a garden dedicated to, and honed by, one of the greatest painters of all time! Life is a paradox.

177

With hearts and souls overflowing, we quietly got into dear old Mistress R. Soul and commanded her to transport us to Le Touquet, and our hotel, which she did. We ate once again at our favourite restaurant, Café des Arts, and slept soundly, our dreams full of colour and sound, of places and people. We breakfasted on our last coffees and croissants and prepared for the final leg to Le Shuttle and England.

After a wonderful week, Gaz and I made a rather quieter journey back, staying overnight in Bourges. We had a lot to think about because somewhere, at some point over the last year, we made the decision that our life in France offers us more *cajones*-grabbing opportunities. This is not a negative against the land of our birth but a positive for the lifestyle we have found. As an ardent Remainer, I've decided to do my own little bit of remaining, for yet another year, especially with my homeland leaving Europe in just over a week. I would never become a French citizen but will remain an *étranger*[2], for a bit longer, if they will let me.

For three months we have negotiated the rental of a villa in the village of Tourbes. Despite assurance from the owners that it would go ahead, personal circumstances forced them to withdraw two weeks before we were due to move. Now we must decide what to do next. Sometimes we feel like children taking our first steps into an unknown future. Not tentatively, but headlong, first one step, then another, hardly looking where we are heading. Recent events have made us determined to try to live life to the fullest while we can. We know that each step will be exciting. And the next. And the next.

Wanna come?

---

2 Foreigner, stranger

45

Well goodness gracious me

December 2019

'Tis around the midnight hour and a figure approaches my bed.
I feel my sheets pulled aside and take a sharp intake of breath
as my pyjama bottoms are pulled open and a mumbling takes
place. I look up to see the figure bending over and peering down
into the pyjama-clad abyss.

I sigh. 'Here we go again.'

Because it is a regular occurrence, I'm getting used to this intrusion. In fact, the other day I realised there was a queue forming to take part in the ritual. Looking for Gaz to question this, I realised he'd donned a medical disguise and was number three in line. Some just look into the dark and mysterious interior that is beyond my pyjama cord; some though, prod and probe and one of them does this really strange thing of bending two fingers into a claw, pressing them into my painful stomach and then beating a tattoo with one finger of the other hand. To what end I have no idea. Perhaps the French, being stretched, have sought support from witch doctors.

Yes, I'm in hospital. Now, the expats extol the virtues of the French healthcare system and I can understand why. There are generally no long waiting lists. I had tummy pain for a few days, saw my local doctor, tried antibiotics which failed to improve the situation and so, on the doctor's advice, turned up unannounced at *Urgences* (our A&E), was assessed, scanned and admitted within three hours and operated on at 9.00 am the following morning. But not without financial implications, my friends. We now have our *Carte Vitale*[1] which entitles us to claim the expenses of treatments which are free at the point of contact, and also 75% of other costs which are retrieved from the British Government. Of course, even 25% of the cost of surgery and two weeks in hospital can add up to many thousands of euros so we, like many others, pay private top-up insurance, at a joint cost of one hundred and fifty-five euros per month. Cancer and heart problems are free to all and for the very poor it is free for everything.

We deliberated long and hard about the extra cost which is financial big bananas for us. We sought the opinion of friends and that opinion was totally divided. We tried to work out how much we might use medical services. Strangely, although I am older than Gazzie (only in years, readers, just years), I appear

---

1 State health insurance card

to be healthier (pause while I touch wood). The longest I've stayed in hospital was overnight to have a baby and that was during the Jurassic Age. We had completed an insurance form but not returned to sign it. We pro'd and con'd for several months until we were passing the insurance office one day and Gaz said, 'I'm going in to sign,' and so we did, and paid our first premium. Just two days before my admittance to hospital. Hospitals, in this area anyway, are modern and clean, seem more than adequately staffed by adorable, young and efficient nursing staff, most of whom try to speak some English. The male doctors are not so keen to try.

So at my age of fragility, I was hospitalised. Everything was new to me. Another set of rules and etiquette to be observed. On my way to the operating theatre I can remember being parked alone in a sort of equipment graveyard – a room full of stretchers with bits falling off, wheelchairs leaning perilously on three wheels and I remember wondering if this was the patients' worth-to-the-world assessment area. Fully awake in a totally silent world, I imagined I was in a sort of purgatory where gods in white coats gave a thumbs up or down to the fate of medical equipment as well as the occasional patient getting towards her use-by date. Before I met my assessors, though, I was back in my private room, sun pouring in the windows, morphine pouring into my arm, and the dearest man in the world peering at me. I must have had the thumbs up by those white-coated judges and was to be allowed a few more years of Prosecco abuse.

I have barely spent a night alone in my life and was worried about being left with no-one except lovely people with little English. I feared I would unknowingly agree to have my organs used for medical experiments while I was still awake and alive, or bits chopped off and replaced to give the staff a bit of practice.

On my first evening, Gazzie said, 'I'd better be going, if I'm to be here tomorrow when you go down for the op.'

181

'OK love,' I said, though my lips were trembling so much it probably sounded like, 'Erby bub.'

And then came a golden angel in a nurse's uniform (this was pre-morphine) who said, 'Please don't cry. Your husband can stay with you if you wish. That's a fold up bed behind you. I'll bring blankets.'

A torrent of the new language I had created poured from my lips:

'Eets bunderbull. Wahlick. Bunderbull.'

Gazzie's face was a bit difficult to read, but I really think he was thrilled at the prospect of sleeping on three bits of plywood for the foreseeable future.

There were compensations for him though. I have told you already that Gazzie likes a uniform and no occasion is too minor for him to don his workman's outfit, policeman's outfit or, my favourite, the fireman. However Gazzie's fave has always been the doctor. Whenever I've got a little cold, on goes the white coat, the professionally kind doctorly face, the shaking of thermometers and pulse-beat counting. Now, my darlings, he had a stage on which to perform. He sits beside me as my vital signs are measured, nodding sagely as numbers, unintelligible to me, pop up in glorious technicolour on the nurses' computer screens. He follows the nurses outside, where murmured conversations take place. In his white coat, he wanders the corridors, fingering an imaginary stethoscope, nodding to other medical professionals in a slightly aloof manner. How he hasn't been arrested for very suspicious behaviour I shall never know. But when he nods encouragingly as nurses tear from me plasters the size of the Bayeux Tapestry with the 'quick is kinder approach', and then very carefully peel me from the ceiling, to be honest, he could perform surgery on me anytime. My own Dr. Kildare.

So. Diagnosis? An abscessed appendix. But both abscess and appendix were removed. Or were they? That evening my surgeon called in. They do this twice a day. Amazing. He looked pretty grave and said a lot of stuff which we didn't understand, but what we did deduce was that he might have to operate again the following day. My perky, brave little face disintegrated and back came the strange, blubbery language.

'Bo, bo do mwore cutty.'

Our English-speaking nurse came in to give us the lowdown on my low downs.

'The doctor thinks there is another abscess. It was hidden in the scan because it's in the Douglas Sac.'

I'm thinking, 'What's that to do with me? Surely Douglas, whoever he is, can remove the thing from his own bag?' Seeing our looks of total confusion, the nurse laughed and explained that most women are blessed with old Douglas's handbag hidden down among their bits. Must say he got around a bit, that man. And then, just as all of that was about to give me another story for this book, the infection disappeared and the process of recuperating began.

And time for me to learn more hospital ways. Have you ever tried to go to the loo whilst attached to a metal plant holder? One-handedly, you wriggle out of bed, one arm attached to a wire and a bottle and the plant holder. You set off, trip over the end of the bed and the bottle jigs around precariously as you try to wheel the whole contraption into the bathroom. How to raise the lid, turn around, lower pyjama bottoms. Well, I'll let your imagination take over, but by the time you achieve your objective it's almost too late and by the time you get back to bed, it's time to set off again.

'If you need anything, press the emergency bell,' the dear nurses say with that professional smile. What it actually means is, 'If you could possibly predict that unbearable pain is going to happen in about an hour's time, ring the bell, and by the time we get to you, we might just about be in time to hook you up to the painkiller.'

And what constitutes an emergency? Not being practised in

the skill of having only one usable arm, the other being hooked up to a bag of liquid pumping its way into me, I did get myself into some pickles when Gaz was unavailable – off gallivanting and eating decent food at McDonald's. I decided I really needed to change my pyjamas, particularly as the poke, prod and look down my pyjama bottoms club was increasing in popularity. So I tried to first work out the technicalities. Then to put them into practice. So you may wonder why I started by removing my pyjama bottoms. The answer, I suppose, is that I'm no good at working out technicalities, and anyway removing them seemed to be the simplest part of the operation: a push with one hand and a bit of a wriggle on the bed and the bottoms were off. Now to remove the sleeve from the unfettered arm. Once I'd managed that, sitting with one sleeve round my neck and barely anything covering my dignity, I looked from the drip bottle to my still-sleeved arm, and back, working out how to extricate one from the other. Right. Unhook bottle of fluid. Remove sleeve from fettered arm. Get bottle to end of sleeve, pull through with pipe. *Voilà. Non!*[2] I now had a sleeve with pipes wound round it tightly, my neck was against the top of the drip stand and I was, in fact, hanging myself, naked. I oscillated my eyes like spinning marbles trying to locate the emergency button. There. I risked snapping my carotid artery stretching to reach it. And pressed. Just as I was about to lose consciousness, the door opened slowly and in walked the only male nurse on our ward.

Chuckling merrily, he took my weight in his arms.

'Hah, that stopped his merry chuckling,' I thought gleefully. 'Taking my weight nearly killed him.'

He unwound and untangled me and returned the drip to its dripping station and me unceremoniously to the bed and left me, still chuckling. Then I realised I still hadn't got clean pyjamas on. In fact, no pyjamas at all.

---

2 There you are. No

184

One of the drips on my multi-branched drip station was liquid food. I rather liked it. No shopping. No preparation. No washing up. But I heard little hints as I began to get better. 'Maybe tomorrow. Real food.' Well, I'm not saying I wasn't a bit excited, especially as it was only the eating bit I was required to do. The three course meal came along. The first course was often on the menu and became known in our little room as 'dog turd soup'. This was a rather complimentary sobriquet for something so completely tasteless. The main course was totally white: a lump of white – maybe fish – and white rice, accompanied by a dessert of mashed Polyfilla. It is inconceivable that even with a restricted budget, anyone could produce something that looked or tasted so unlike food.

My darling daughter flew over without telling us, hired a car so Gazzie wouldn't have to drive her around and poked her dear, sweet face around my room door.

'Hello Mummy.'

And she brought the sunshine in, hung up her illuminated climbing Santa and said, 'Sleep now.' She distance-worked on her computer while I slept and a party started later when Gazzie, the evening shift nurses and the pyjama lifters all arrived at once. She took Gazzie out for some proper food and then went back to our cold little house to sleep alone. She made me start walking and took me out to the front of the hospital in my sparkly slippers to feel hot winter sunshine on our faces. My recovery rate escalated by about one hundred percent. How lucky I am to have her and dear Gazzie who, despite a back lacerated by the put-you-up, his body mired with lack of sleep, raced around in the daytime and joined me in the evening for a film on the iPad thing.

Sitting here at home, after eleven days in hospital, I smile. Despite much pain, no television and diabolical food, my experience was not an unhappy one. Nurses will visit me here every day for as long as the wound takes to heal. A hellish time for me with no baths, but I am not complaining. Gaz is out getting the Christmas tree. We'll dress it tonight. We'll light the fire and, I'm thinking, maybe, just maybe, he can put on his doctor's uniform. Just because.

46

Where Do We Go From Here?

March 2020

The church bells make a solemn, funereal sound over the village. It is midday on 17th March 2020.

'Allo, Allo,' says the public address system and informs the already spooked villagers to go into their houses and stay there. To be protected from COVID-19. It's like a scene from a sci-fi film, without the handsome hero who will save a few attractive women of childbearing age including the pretty, busty nurse he met somewhere during the opening titles. I've just got Gaz.

Speaking of Gazzie, as I so often do, sad old bird that I am, he can find the positive in any situation. Hunting/gathering is fraught with danger at the moment as supermarkets become possible danger zones for the spread of the virus. Gaz has found a solution and you won't be surprised to learn it involves a uniform. Somewhere he's found a deep sea diver's suit (circa 1920) complete with brass helmet. He dons this outfit to go to the supermarket every day. Did you know that in those days the boots were made of something like concrete? (I suppose to pull 1920s divers to the bottom of the sea.) It is jolly hard work to wear this lot and push a trolley containing five hundred toilet rolls and fifty tins of bloaters. I expect I will hate bloaters – some sort of marine life I believe – but it's all that's left in the shop and we're not ones to look gift fish in the mouth. It'll be gift horses next. The horse meat van still visits the village once a week. And why toilet rolls, when this particular virus does not appear to attack one's nether regions?

All over France, husbands, wives and children are locked in their houses for two weeks initially, but probably longer. If the divorce rate goes up over the few confinement days of Christmas, will anyone still be married after months of this?

And have you noticed the barely-contained glee of the three-year-old newsreaders who daily intone that the disease is mainly fatal for the over-seventies with underlying health problems? I'm doomed, Mr. Mainwaring. Doomed.

And so we make brave little resolutions: to get fresh air we shall eat our breakfast on the balcony each day, followed by a half-hour exercise routine starting with raising one finger at a time for five minutes and progressing slowly through to all our digits. We're hoping that will take us to July when it will be too hot for movement of any kind.

Towards the end of the day, weary and aching from all the activity, I am sure we'll take time, over a little *apéritif* on that bloomin' balcony, to reflect on our two and a bit years here and

188

to decide what to do next. Wherever we are, one thing is for sure: we'll get a much bigger balcony. The one here is about four feet by ten feet. Not enough on which two can comfortably breakfast, exercise, lunch, post-lunch snooze, tea, have a quick game of table tennis and then discuss their future over a glass (or five) before dinner.

It seems to me that this book you are reading, those of you who are still with me, personifies what has happened to me during these years in France. That journey south from my settled life in England gave me permission to change myself, to be whatever was possible. Ah, maybe that is it. Possibilities not inevitabilities. And so it is in France that I, a life-long reader, will realise my life-long dream of publishing a book that I have written. I will hold it in my hand on my eightieth birthday. Not, 'Never say never,' but, '*Ne jamais dire jamais.*'

What has particularly thrilled me is the ability to make new friendships at my age: good, strong, loyal friendships. You don't have to know someone all your life to consider them a friend. Immigrants have honed the ability to cut away the superficial dross and go straight to the essence. I have always believed that we shouldn't love for looks, or intelligence or station, but for the very heart of each and every one. It gives me faith in humanity that the mantra for this strangest of years is, 'Be kind.' Though not all countries speak English.

A month ago, we were planning a trip back to the UK to surprise our daughter on Mother's Day, as she has surprised me on so many occasions. We had booked and paid for Le Shuttle and hotels in Île de Ré and Le Touquet, dinners with friends in Whitstable, and quality time with family. And I had hoped for adventures to share with you, dear readers. But it became obvious, as various European countries started to restrict travel due to the rapid spread of the Coronavirus, that this was not a sensible idea, and so we made cancellations. As it happens, all but essential travel is now forbidden. I was completely devastated. Despite this life-enhancing existence that I have shared with you over the last few years, I still ache for the mostly grey skies and pebble beaches of Whitstable, the amazing restaurants, the incomparable sunsets, being known by the shopkeepers, and being loved by, and loving, my friends. Oh, London – I see you on the television and yearn for you, city of my homesick dreams. I miss your bustling streets, your multicultural residents, your theatres, your museums, the grace of your architecture and the enduring thrill of leaving the train at St. Pancras and falling into your dusty, familiar arms. And my family – oh, my family – they more than all of the rest:

Can we pop in for a cup of tea?

Can we come over with our new boyfriend/girlfriend?

We're having a party, Mum, wanna come?

The circle that grows ever wider: the family, their friends, the children of their friends, the friends of their children. And us at the centre of that circle, part of it and protected by it.

So, however long this *lockdown, self-isolation, lock up the old 'uns* lasts, I suspect Gazzie and I will not stop debating, 'Where do we go from here?' Do we go back home to the familiar, to the family and all that is within our comfort zone, or do we make our home in France with its soft borders, its opportunities, its challenges? Like the essence of loving that I write about here, the choice for me is an emotional one. Where does my heart lie? We cannot live in both worlds. I know Gary has made his choice, which makes it doubly hard for me. He is unquestioningly happy here in this beautiful country with its blue hills, its vines, its unspoilt beaches and its boar-mangled golf course.

And me? I'm stuck at the crossroads, loving the view in both directions . . . but which route will I take?